The Open University

T224

Computers and processors

Block 1
Introduction to hardware, software and data

Authors: Bernie Clark and Mirabelle Walker

This publication forms part of an Open University course T224 *Computers and processors*. Details of this and other Open University courses can be obtained from the Student Registration and Enquiry Service, The Open University, PO Box 197, Milton Keynes MK7 6BJ, United Kingdom: tel. +44 (0)870 333 4340, email general-enquiries@open.ac.uk

Alternatively, you may visit the Open University website at http://www.open.ac.uk where you can learn more about the wide range of courses and packs offered at all levels by The Open University.

To purchase a selection of Open University course materials visit the webshop at www.ouw.co.uk, or contact Open University Worldwide, Michael Young Building, Walton Hall, Milton Keynes MK7 6AA, United Kingdom for a brochure. tel. +44 (0)1908 858785; fax +44 (0)1908 858787; e-mail ouwenq@open.ac.uk

The Open University
Walton Hall, Milton Keynes
MK7 6AA

First published 2005. Second edition 2007.

Typeset in India by Alden Prepress Services, Chennai

Printed and bound in the United Kingdom by Hobbs the Printers Limited, Brunel Road, Totton, Hampshire SO40 3WX

ISBN 978 0 7492 2336 6

2.1

Contents

1 **Introduction**

Computers have become a vital part of everyday life. It is almost inconceivable that you could spend a day without at least one event being influenced by a computer. Perhaps the word 'computer' automatically conjures up the image of a personal computer sitting on a desk, but in fact it is the computers you cannot see that influence your life the most. Typical examples of common products that may use these 'invisible' computers are:

> cars
>
> washing machines
>
> bar-code reading systems
>
> DVD players/writers
>
> central-heating controllers
>
> microwave ovens
>
> games consoles.

This is a very short extract from a very long list, but even this limited set of examples shows how significant the use of computers has become. Without computers many everyday products such as mobile phones and personal digital assistants (PDAs) would not exist, dramatic progress in the development of products such as artificial limbs could not have happened, and you would not have the luxury of many conveniences now taken for granted, such as e-mail.

The computers which form the basis of those used today were mainly developed in the 1940s. The following quote taken from that era shows how difficult it was to conceive of the way in which computers would develop in the following decades.

> I think there is a world market for maybe five computers.
>
> (Thomas Watson, Chairman of IBM, 1943)

Even later on, in the mid 1970s, some still failed to comprehend the size of the future computer market.

> There is no reason for any individual to have a computer in his home.
>
> (Ken Olsen, President of Digital Equipment Corporation, 1977)

And although a diminution in size was anticipated, it was considerably underestimated.

> Where a calculator on the ENIAC is equipped with 18 000 vacuum tubes and weighs 30 tons, computers in the future may have only 1000 vacuum tubes and perhaps weigh $1\frac{1}{2}$ tons.
>
> (*Popular Mechanics*, March 1949)

Figure 1 shows a picture of the ENIAC computer mentioned above. You can see it is rather larger than the personal computer available today! Completed in the US in 1945, it was one of the earliest electronic computers. Its name stands for Electronic Numerical Integrator And

Calculator, and it was designed to calculate ballistic firing tables in the Second World War. It could perform mathematical operations such as addition, subtraction, multiplication and division, and it could find the square root and compare two values for equality.

Figure 1 The ENIAC computer

As part of the ENIAC fiftieth anniversary celebrations, students and staff at the University of Pennsylvania fabricated a version of this computer using modern manufacturing processes. The component at the heart of this later version measures 7.44 millimetres by 5.29 millimetres! A personal computer was connected to this component to provide the modern equivalent of the cable connections shown on the left hand side of Figure 1 and display the ENIAC's outputs.

Computers like ENIAC were built because of the need for powerful automatic calculators. Another famous use for an early computer was the work at Bletchley Park in the UK to break the German diplomatic codes used in the Second World War.

computer
input device

A **computer** is a machine that manipulates data following a list of instructions that have been programmed into it. **Input devices** are used to input data into a computer; the keyboard of a personal computer, the scanner of a bar-code reading system and the switches or buttons of a microwave oven are some examples. The list of instructions the computer

computer program

follows is called a **computer program**. So, for example, a bar-code reader that sends the name of a scanned bar-coded product to a display will have been programmed with a set of instructions that makes it:

- take in data via the bar-code scanner;
- use the data from the bar-code scanner to look up the name of the product in a list that cross references bar-code data to product name;
- generate a new form of data that is compatible with showing the product name on the display;

- send the newly generated data to the display to show the product name.

In this example the display is being used as an **output device**. There are many different types of output device. The actuator that switches on a pump of a computer-controlled central-heating system is one example; the sound system that generates the beep of an electronic heart monitor is another.

output device

I have used the word 'data' several times now in the context of the computer receiving input data, generating data and outputting data. A computer can only work with information that is presented to it in a very strictly controlled format. When information is in this format it is called data. Quite simply, a computer cannot perform its task if the information it needs has not been transformed into the required data form. You will find out more about the format of data a computer needs later on in this block.

As computers have developed, a critical change in their role has been their use in communication: many of the applications that run on personal computers (PCs) help us communicate with each other, and also with other computers. The following quote from Danny Hillis, a pioneer in the development of some of the fastest and most powerful computers, gives some insight into how computers can turn everyday objects into part of a communication system.

> I went to my first computer conference at the New York Hilton about 20 years ago. When somebody there predicted the market for microprocessors [these are the major component of all computers] would eventually be in the millions, someone else said, 'Where are they all going to go? It's not like you need a computer in every doorknob!' Years later, I went back to the same hotel. I noticed the room keys had been replaced by electronic cards you slide into slots in the doors.
>
> There was a computer in every doorknob.
>
> (Danny Hillis, circa 1999)

Of course you do not know exactly the configuration of the computers in the doorknobs of the Hilton; it could be that they simply verified that the card should give the holder access to that particular room. Alternatively the doorknob computer could communicate with another computer, telling it that the occupant had just entered the room. This second computer could then ring the telephone to pass on any recorded messages, activate a display showing if the occupant had received any e-mail or perhaps run the bath!

As you study this course you will find out how computers and the components within them carry out their allotted tasks, and you will also develop an understanding of how improvements in computer technologies have allowed computers to become smaller, more powerful and cheaper.

2 Computers and computer systems

Figure 2 shows an advertisement for a personal computer (PC) published in February 2004. The main features of the computer are listed in this advert. The first item on the list is 'Intel® Pentium® 4 Processor 2.80 GHz'. So this computer uses an Intel Pentium 4 Processor, running at a speed of 2.80 GHz. A **processor** is an essential component of a computer; it carries out or **executes** the instructions that make up the computer program. PCs use one main processor and several other 'supporting' processors, and adverts for PCs often specify what main processor they use. The speed of the processor (2.80 GHz in this instance) is a measure of how fast the processor can carry out each instruction. (Don't worry if you don't understand the term 'GHz' and other specialised terms used in the advert such as '512 MB DDR RAM'. These will be explained as the course progresses.)

processor
execute

Figure 2 An advertisement for a personal computer

microprocessor

You may remember that the quote from Danny Hillis in Section 1 mentioned a microprocessor. The term **microprocessor** was introduced when processors were first made on a single silicon chip, with the prefix 'micro' emphasising their small size. Today, however, the fact that a processor can be made on a single silicon chip is taken for granted and the term 'microprocessor' is not so often used. This course will generally use the term 'processor'.

All computers, not just PCs, contain processors, so all those 'invisible' computers I listed earlier will contain a processor. However, the processor they use will not necessarily be the same as that used in a PC. For example, the processor used within a central-heating controller would not be the same as the main processor used in the personal computer you are using to study this course. The processor in the personal computer has to carry out a much more complex set of tasks and execute its instructions much more quickly than the processor in the central heating controller. As a result the PC's processor is likely to be physically larger and more costly. However you will see later in the course that the complexity and speed of operation of processors has increased dramatically. As a result, the 'simple' processor in an electronic central heating controller may be very similar to a processor which was considered 'state of the art' a decade or two previously.

You should now be beginning to build up a picture of what a computer is: you know it needs input and output devices to communicate with the world outside and a processor to carry out the instructions that are programmed into it. But where are these instructions stored within the computer? The answer is that they are stored within what is called the computer's **main memory**, along with any data needed to carry them out.

main memory

However, the main memory in computers like PCs is much too small to hold all of the programs and associated data that their users need. In addition, main memory does not hold onto its contents when the computer is switched off. So users must be able to call up the programs they want, and also store and read back the files they have generated with these programs, from some form of capacious and retentive memory. This memory is called **secondary memory**, and there are two types, removable and permanent. With removable secondary memory the user can store files and then 'remove' them from the PC, either to ensure there are copies if the computer fails, or to transport the files to another PC. New software can also be installed from removable secondary memory. Removable secondary memory includes floppy disks, CD-ROMs, memory cards and DVDs. In contrast, permanent secondary memory is 'permanently' attached to the PC and is usually only removed if the PC is undergoing some maintenance or repair. A typical example of permanent secondary memory is a computer's **hard disk** – so called because it consists of one or more rigid magnetic disks rotating about a central axle. It is common practice to copy the files stored on permanent secondary memory onto some removable secondary memory as a backup in case of disk failure.

secondary memory

hard disk

Although programs and associated data are stored on the hard disk when not actually in use, both the programs and the data must be copied into the computer's main memory before the processor can execute the instructions or use the data.

The third and fourth items in the list of features of the PC in Figure 2 show that this PC has 512 MB of main memory and a hard drive that provides 80 GB of secondary memory. Note that I used the term 'hard disk', but in the advert the term 'hard drive' is used to refer to the permanent secondary memory. These terms are often used synonymously, though in fact there is a subtle difference which I'll explain shortly. (Remember that other specialised terms associated with the computer's features will be explained as the course progresses.)

Activity 1 (Exploratory)

What other secondary memory device or devices are used by the PC in the advert shown in Figure 2?

Comment

Item 7 on the list of features shows that the PC also uses DVDs and CDs as removable secondary memory.

All computers have main memory, but not all will have secondary memory. In an 'invisible' computer such as the central-heating controller, the software is already stored in the main memory when the computer is purchased. The software is said to be already installed. The PC you are using on this course will have come with some software already installed on it – the software the PC needs to start up when you switch it on. But a key difference between an 'invisible' computer like the one in the central-heating controller and the PC is that users cannot install any additional software on the 'invisible' computer, whereas they can and do install their own choice of software onto a PC. They do this by copying computer programs into the secondary memory, as you will do when you install the T224 course software. Such programs are then taken into the main memory when the program is run.

So far, I have introduced the major components of a computer, namely a processor along with input and output devices, plus main and secondary memory. I now want to explore three of these components a little further, starting with input devices.

Input devices have to collect some information from outside the computer and present it to the computer as data[1] which is in a form the processor can work with. It is useful to think of these as two separate functions:

- 'capturing' the information;
- 'translating' the information into a data form the processor can use.

Sometimes these two functions are done by a single physical entity; sometimes by two separate entities. When I am talking about input functions I shall use the term you have already met, 'input device', for **input subsystem**   whatever *captures* the information and the term **input subsystem** for whatever does the *translation*.

Similarly, output devices have to collect data from the processor in the processor's format and translate it into something that is meaningful outside the computer, and again it's useful to think of these as two separate functions:

- 'translating' from the data form the processor uses;
- 'presenting' the information.

Again, when I am talking about output functions I shall use the term 'output device' for whatever *presents* the information and the term **output subsystem**   **output subsystem** for whatever does the *translation*.

In the case of secondary memory, there are also two functions, though they are rather different. The secondary memory's function is simply to

---

[1] Strictly speaking, 'data' is the plural of the Latin word 'datum'. But in the world of computers 'data' is very often used in the singular, and this course follows that practice.

hold stored data, and a **secondary memory subsystem** is used to *prepare* the data for storage and get it stored (when data is being sent to the memory) or to collect stored data and prepare that data for use by the processor (when data is being sent from the memory). Here is the subtle difference between 'hard disk' and 'hard drive' that I mentioned earlier: the hard disk is the secondary memory and the hard drive is the secondary memory subsystem. But remember that many people use the two synonymously (and hence ambiguously). Often the subtle distinction doesn't matter in a particular context, but it's worth being alert to the fact that the two terms are not strictly synonymous.

secondary memory subsystem

The diagram in Figure 3 shows all the functional blocks of a computer. That is, it shows all the *functions* performed within a computer. Some of the components in any particular example of a computer may perform more than one of the functions shown in Figure 3, so there may not always be a separate physical entity associated with each function shown in the diagram. For example, sometimes an output device and its associated output subsystem are housed together; in some small computers the processor and the main memory are even housed together. But, with the possible exception of secondary memory, any computer will have the functionality shown in Figure 3.

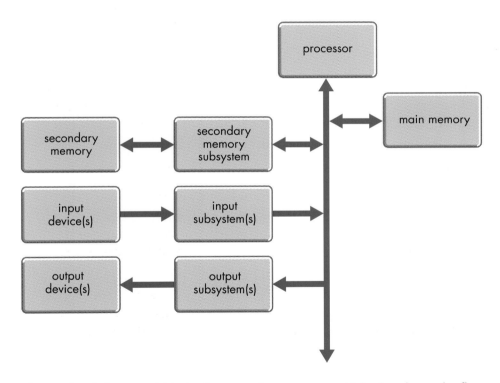

Figure 3 A functional block diagram of a computer which also shows the flow of data within the computer

In Figure 3 the interconnecting lines show the data flows. The thick line running vertically down the page from the processor represents the **computer bus**. This is a data path that connects the input and output subsystems and the secondary memory subsystem to the computer's processor and main memory. It allows data to be transmitted from one part of the computer to another. Notice that this path has an arrow at each end, indicating that data can travel in both directions along it. The arrows on the other paths indicate that data can also travel both to and

computer bus

from the secondary memory, but data only travels in from the input devices and out to the output devices.

Figure 3 is an important diagram, and you will see it, and variations of it, again later in the course. Figure 3 illustrates the fact that computers, however complex and 'clever' they may seem, do only the following tasks:

- *receive* data from the outside world via their input devices;
- *store* that data in their memory;
- *manipulate* that data in their processor, probably creating and storing more data while doing so;
- *present* data back to the outside world via their output devices.

As I have already mentioned, the functional blocks shown in Figure 3 relate very closely to, even though they are not necessarily identical with, the computer's physical components. The computer's physical components are normally known collectively as the **hardware**. **Software** is a term often used to refer to a computer program or a collection of computer programs which enable a computer to carry out its tasks. As the course progresses you will find out a great deal about computer hardware and software, including the processor and the programs it runs. You will generate some programs yourself and look at the operation of the processor to see how it executes the instructions within them. Through this you will gain an understanding of what form the data used by the processor and memory must take, and hence understand the role of the input and output subsystems.

hardware
software

digital

binary

Electrical signals and computers

The data that travels along the main computer bus does so in the form of electrical signals which can have one of two possible values: a near-zero voltage, known as 'voltage low', and a rather higher voltage, probably around 3 volts[2], known as 'voltage high'. Any electrical signal where the number of possible values that can be used is limited is known as a **digital** signal. If the number of possible values is limited to just two, as on the computer bus, then the signal is known as a **binary** digital signal, or simply a binary signal. (The 'bi' in 'binary' means 'two'.)

So the electrical signals that travel along the computer bus, and hence to the output subsystems and from the input subsystems, are all binary signals. Unfortunately, the electrical signals produced by input devices or needed by output devices are not necessarily binary, or even digital. Hence an important task of the input and output subsystems is to transform between the binary signals on the computer bus and whatever signals are used by their particular input or output device.

---

[2] This is the voltage used to represent a '1' that is most common at the time of writing (early 2004). A couple of decades ago the value was usually nearer to 5 volts, and older systems still use this value. Some newer systems are already using voltages near 2 volts and this may well become the most common value in a few years.

Activity 2 (Self assessment)

For the PC shown in Figure 2, write down which of the functional blocks in Figure 3 the following items of hardware relate to (for simplicity, items that provide input functionality can be assumed to relate to input devices, rather than input subsystems, and similarly for items that provide output functionality):

Keyboard, monitor, 80 GB hard drive, 512 MB DDR RAM, speakers, mouse, DVD and CD.

Comment

The answer is at the end of Block 1.

Activity 3 (Exploratory)

The following items are listed under the features of the PC shown in Figure 2: a sound card and a modem. What problem arises if you try to relate these two items to the functional blocks of Figure 3?

Comment

The problem is that the sound card is used for *both* input and output (it takes inputs from a microphone and delivers outputs to one or more speakers). The modem is also used for both input and output (it both sends signals to and receives signals from the telephone network). Therefore these items do not at first seem to fit neatly with Figure 3. But remember that the diagram is showing *functionality*. So you can relate the input functionality of the sound card to the 'input subsystem' item in Figure 3 (the microphone would be the input device), and the output functionality of the sound card to the 'output subsystem' (the speaker or speakers would be the output device). In the case of the modem its input functionality relates to the 'input device' in Figure 3, and its output functionality to the 'output device'.

The terms **input–output device** and **input–output subsystem** are sometimes used where items have both input and output functionality. Hence a sound card is an input–output subsystem.

input–output device
input–output subsystem

Finally, just as you are just becoming familiar with all of the terms I have been introducing, I need to add a word of caution. When you read books or other literature about computers you may find some of the terms I have defined used differently. This is not necessarily a problem, and is common when technical terms become part of everyday language. However, throughout your study of T224 you do need to make sure that you use the terms as defined here, so that your understanding and the teaching of the course team are in harmony.

One term I have not used here that you might come across is **computer system**. Historically some people used the terms 'computer' and 'computer system' rather differently. But that is no longer the case, and nowadays the word 'system' tends to be omitted. A good example is the use of the term 'personal computer', which would several years ago have often been described as a 'personal computer system'.

computer system

3 Some facts about processors

In this section you are going to find out a little more about one of the key components of a computer: the processor, which manipulates data according to a list of instructions called a program.

3.1 Processor statistics

Here is a mini-quiz which explores some facts about processors.

Question 1

Which of the numbers given below is closest to the number of processors sold worldwide in 2000?

A   20 million   B   40 million
C   125 million   D   1 billion

Question 2

Which of the numbers given below is closest to the number of processors installed in a BMW 7-series car in 1999?

A   1   B   5
C   100   D   5000

Question 3

Which of the numbers given below is closest to the number of processors you own?

A   1   B   4
C   50   D   1000

Answers

Question 1

The answer to Question 1 is D. The processor market is vast; it is estimated that around 1 billion processors were sold in 2000.

Question 2

The correct answer is C, 100 processors. The BMW 7-series manufactured in 1999 uses 65 processors. Not all these are used in the engine management system; for example the processor in the automatic transmission communicates with the processors behind each side view mirror, so they tilt down and inward whenever the driver puts the car into reverse gear. Also the processor in the car radio communicates with the processors controlling the brakes so the audio volume can be adjusted to compensate for additional road noise resulting from the application of the brakes.

Question 3

Perhaps your answer to this will vary from mine, which is C, 50 processors. If you answered A, just one processor, you may have been thinking about the PC you are using to study this course. However, in addition to their main processor PCs contain at least another seven processors, as you will find out later in the course. You also need to consider the domestic products you may own. There are processors in some toasters, washing machines, home entertainment systems, tumble dryers, central-heating controllers, video and DVD players, microwave ovens, electronic clocks, TVs, children's toys, computer games, phones, satellite systems and so on, and of course remember the ones you may have in your car. I quite quickly identified around 30 processors that I own, and if I thought about it for longer I would probably find a few more, but it was obvious that the total would be much less than answer D, 1000 processors.

Perhaps you got all the answers to the quiz correct; perhaps all your answers were wrong. It doesn't matter. What is important is that you now appreciate:

- the huge number of applications that can use processors and hence how vast the processor market is;
- that the market for processors is not limited to personal computers;
- and that the market for processors used in personal computers is very much smaller than that for processors used in other applications.

3.2 What does a processor look like?

So what do these devices that are manufactured in such vast quantities look like? Processors are manufactured as integrated circuits. You will find out more about these in Block 4, but essentially they are circuits, around the size of a fingernail, which contain many millions of electronic components manufactured as one very complex circuit. Figure 4(a) shows how a processor manufactured as an integrated circuit is packaged so it can be used as a component in an electronic circuit. The pins of the package are connected to the integrated circuit using gold[3] bonding wire. Some of the pins are used to supply the electrical power to the device, while signals are input to and output from the processor via other pins. Figure 4(c) shows the integrated circuit I mentioned in Section 1, the one developed as part of the ENIAC fiftieth anniversary project.

Figure 5 shows the packaged processor assembled with other components on the motherboard of a computer. A motherboard is the major circuit board inside a computer and it holds the processor, the computer bus, the main memory and many other vital components.

---

[3] Gold is most commonly used, but sometimes aluminium is used instead.

Enlarged area

Gold wire bonded to the integrated circuit runs under the ceramic to connect to the pins

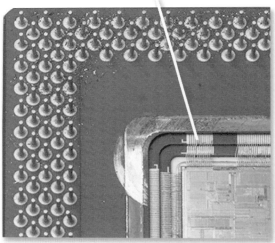

Underside of a packaged processor

(a)

Cover removed to expose the integrated circuit and connecting wires

(b)

(c)

Figure 4   (a) The inside of a packaged processor; (b) detail of the integrated circuit and connecting wires; (c) the integrated circuit created as part of the ENIAC fiftieth anniversary project

Figure 5   A processor assembled on a motherboard along with other circuit components

Representing data and instructions inside a computer

I have just indicated that a processor is made up of millions of electronic components manufactured as one very complex circuit. The majority of these components act as switches that can exist in one of only two states, either on or off. The states of certain switches tell the processor what instructions to carry out. Also when a processor is running a program it is altering the state of other switches, switching them on and off many, many times a second.

To represent more easily what is happening to the states of these switches, the 'off' state is often referred to as 0, and the 'on' state as 1.

Imagine eight switches in the following states:

on   off   off   off   on   on   on   off

The states of these switches can be written down concisely as the 8-digit code 10001110, where the digit on the extreme left represents the state of the leftmost switch and so on through to the digit on the extreme right representing the state of the rightmost switch.

If, for example, the state of these switches at any time represented an instruction for a processor to execute, then 10001110 would cause one particular instruction to be executed and 10100001 another. (Later on in the course you will find out how these instructions are represented in shorthand, so a list of instructions doesn't have to be tediously written down as many 1s and 0s.)

The code 10001110 is made up of 8 digits. In computing terminology, because each digit can only take one of two values (either 1 or 0), each digit is referred to as a 'binary digit'. This is almost always abbreviated to **bit**. Therefore I can say 10001110 is an 8-bit code. As the code is in binary it is termed a **binary code**, so 10001110 is an 8-bit binary code.

bit
binary code

Three switches in the following states would represent the 3-bit binary code 100:

on   off   off

Activity 4 (Exploratory)

Write down as many 2-bit binary codes as you can think of.

Comment

There are four possible 2-bit binary codes: 00, 01, 10 and 11.

This representation using 1s and 0s is very convenient. It makes it possible to write down what conditions exist inside the processor without having to deal with the complexities of the voltages and currents that exist to make the switches enter their on and off states. (If you could peer inside a processor you would not see 1s and 0s written down!)

Using binary codes is a very easy way to describe the state of the switches inside the processor, and allows people to represent what the electronic circuits that make up the processor are doing without having to understand how such circuits operate.

But if all the data and computer instructions within a computer are represented by 1s and 0s, how can this limited set of conditions be used to represent, for instance, every letter of the alphabet that might be typed into a computer from a keyboard? Activity 4 showed that there are four possible combinations of 1s and 0s in a 2-bit binary code. So if you had only two bits available you could only represent four different letters e.g. 'a' could be represented by 00, 'b' by 01, 'c' by 10 and 'd' by 11. This shows that a 2-bit binary code can only represent four items of data.

Activity 5 (Self assessment)

Write down all the possible combinations of a 3-bit binary code and state how many items of data three bits can represent.

Comment

The answer is at the end of Block 1.

Interestingly, a pattern can be deduced for the relationship between the number of bits and the number of items they represent.

$$2 \text{ bits can represent } 2 \times 2 = 2^2 = 4 \text{ items}$$
$$3 \text{ bits can represent } 2 \times 2 \times 2 = 2^3 = 8 \text{ items}$$

and following on with the same pattern

$$4 \text{ bits can represent } 2 \times 2 \times 2 \times 2 = 2^4 = 16 \text{ items.}$$

> *Study note: If you are unsure of the use of the mathematical notation 2^2, 2^3 etc. you will find it helpful to refer to the T224 Numeracy Resource.*

byte　　A group of eight bits is called a **byte**, so an 8-bit binary code is 1 byte long, a 16-bit binary code is 2 bytes long and a 64-bit binary code is 8 bytes long.

Activity 6 (Self assessment)

(a) How many bits are there in 4 bytes?

(b) How many items of data can be represented by 1 byte?

Comment

The answer is at the end of Block 1.

In general, computers that perform more complex tasks at higher speeds use a larger number of bits to represent their data and instructions. The very simple central heating controller, which only has to do a limited amount of processing, may use an 8-bit representation. More powerful computers will use 16-, 32- or 64-bit representations.

Later in this block you will find out about the convention that uses an 8-bit binary code to represent the letters of the alphabet plus all the other characters that can be typed from the keyboard of a personal computer.

When a computer is running a program a lot of data is being passed around the various elements within the system. The data received by the input subsystem(s) must be passed to the processor in a form it can use, and the processor in turn must present data to the output subsystem(s) in the required format. Even more fundamentally, the processor must be able to recognise each instruction within the program and execute it. You will explore how all this happens in Block 2 when you use the course's simulated processor to run instructions and manipulate data.

5 Examples of computers

In this section you will look at three different examples of computers: a PC, which is obviously a computer, and a set of electronic kitchen scales and a digital camera, which are not so obviously computers. You will find that all three of these examples match with the functional block diagram of a computer given in Figure 3 in Section 2, although the tasks they have to perform mean that the individual components which perform the functions of the blocks within the diagram are quite different.

5.1 The personal computer

In Activities 2 and 3 you looked at how the components of the PC in Figure 2 could be related to the functional block diagram in Figure 3. Figure 6, which is a functional block diagram for the PC and shows the data flow between the components of the PC in Figure 2, should remind you of the outcome. Notice that in this diagram I have put in specific input and output devices and specific items of secondary memory instead of the generic items of Figure 3. In other words, Figure 3 is a *generic* diagram for any computer; Figure 6 is its *specific* form for the PC of Figure 2.

Other PCs may have some additional input devices such as a web cam, plus some additional output devices such as a printer.

The PC is a general-purpose computer. It can run different software programs at the user's request, and hence can be used for a variety of different applications. Typical examples are word processing, sending and receiving e-mail, playing games, browsing the Web and sound and image recording and playback.

The following quote from the book *A Shortcut through Time, The Path to Quantum Computing* by George Johnson shows that even those long familiar with the concepts of how PCs work can still find them fascinating. (A register is a part of a processor and you will find out about these in Block 2; the term 'disk drive' is often used to describe either a floppy disk or hard disk.)

> With a modern PC we blithely double-click an icon on the desktop summoning a flow of data from the disk drive – the pattern of bits that configures thousands of little switches to act as a word processor or a web browser or an MP3 player – temporary little structures, virtual machines. They are allowed to exist only as long as they are needed. Then they are wiped away and replaced with other structures, all built from 1s and 0s.
>
> It is hard to believe sometimes how well this works. You can call up a movie trailer in a window and drag the image around the desktop, causing millions of bits to pour through the computer's hidden registers. It is overwhelming to try and imagine the precise co-ordination going on behind the screen. Ultimately though it all comes down to shuffling 1s and 0s, flipping little switches on and off.
>
> (George Johnson, *A Shortcut through Time, The Path to Quantum Computing*, 2003)

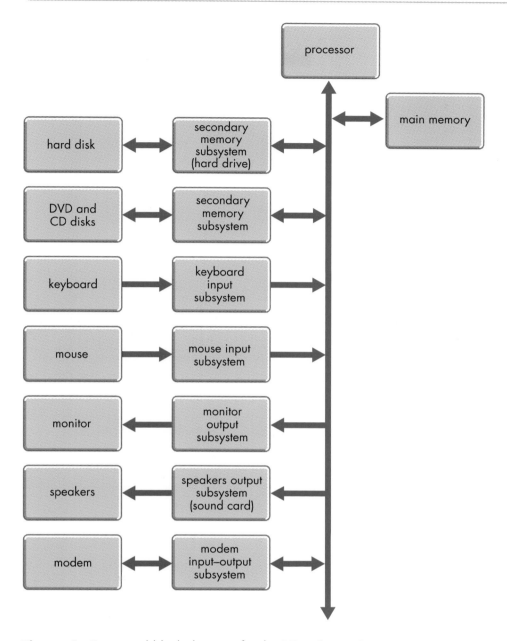

Figure 6 Functional block diagram for the PC in Figure 2

Earlier you looked at how data can be represented by bits – two bits can represent four items, three bits eight items, four bits sixteen items, etc. This is fine if, for example, you want to represent a clearly defined set of data such as the letters of the alphabet and numbers. But how are the images of the 'movie trailer' in the above quote represented in your computer? How can you turn your image into items that can be represented by bits? As you will see from the next two examples, electronic kitchen scales and a digital camera, this issue of data representation exists in all computers and is something you will study in detail later in this block and again in Block 3. You will also study PCs in more detail in Block 4.

5.2 Electronic kitchen scales

A set of electronic kitchen scales is shown in Figure 7. Their basic operation is relatively simple. When they are switched on and, for example, a 500-gram object is placed in the scalepan, the display shows the digits 500 and the letter g.

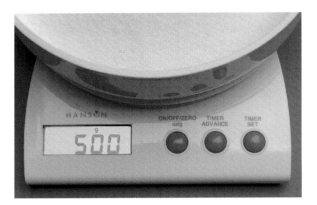

Figure 7   Set of scales showing a reading of 500 g

It might be possible to think of these electronic kitchen scales as a computer, in the sense that that they have hardware in the form of a processor, memory, input devices and subsystems, output devices and subsystems; and they have software in the form of programs. But they are not normally thought of in such terms because the fact that they are a computer is not of primary concern to the user – it seems more natural to think of them as kitchen scales. The term **embedded computer** is sometimes used when a computer is 'hidden' in this way. Objects like the kitchen scales are said to 'contain' a computer, rather than to 'be' a computer – the computer is thought of as being 'embedded' in the object.

embedded computer

For the electronic kitchen scales, a key input device is a sensor placed beneath the scalepan. This sensor measures how far the scalepan moves when an object is placed on it, and generates a signal to represent this change of position. The sensor's subsystem then converts this signal into binary coded data (that is, a pattern of 1s and 0s) that the processor can read and manipulate.

The seven-segment display on the scales is an output device. Its subsystem takes binary coded data from the processor and manipulates it into another binary form that will make the correct digits and letter appear on the display.

The processor in this system is performing a very simple task. Whenever the scales are switched on the program installed in the computer's main memory at manufacture runs. This program first instructs the processor to pick up the data placed on the computer bus by the input subsystem. The program then tells the processor to use this data, plus some data stored in main memory, to generate some further data. This new data is then taken from the bus by the output subsystem.

The computer is essentially taking a signal in one format from the sensor and translating it into another format which enables the display to show the correct digits and letter. It is important that it does this in a time-span acceptable to the user.

Just as Figure 6 is the specific form of the generic diagram in Figure 3 for the PC, so it is possible to create the specific form of Figure 3 for these electronic kitchen scales.

Activity 7 (Self assessment)

Using the information about the scales given above, create the specific form of Figure 3 for the kitchen scales. Note that these scales have no secondary memory.

Comment

The answer is at the end of Block 1.

In products such as these electronic kitchen scales the capabilities of the processor can be used to implement additional features. In this case the scales have a count-down timer so they can be used as a kitchen timer, and they can measure in imperial units (pounds and ounces) as well as metric units. They also implement an add-and-weigh function which allows the user to set the scales' display to zero when there are some ingredients in the scalepan, making it possible to weigh the next ingredient without having to perform any mental arithmetic to add its weight to that of the ingredients already in the scalepan.

Activity 8 (Exploratory)

How might the input and output devices of the scales have to change if a countdown timer, a choice of measuring units and an add-and-weigh feature are all to be implemented? How would this change the diagram you drew for Activity 7?

Comment

The user would need some way of setting the timer, of telling the system whether measurements have to be displayed in imperial or metric, and of switching on and off the add-and-weigh feature. Input buttons would be needed for each of these tasks: to set the timer, change the system between metric and imperial and operate the add-and-weigh function.

A beeper would be needed, to sound when the timer has counted down to zero. The output display would have to have additional functionality; for instance, it would have to show 'oz' and 'lb' for ounces and pounds.

Additional input and output devices and their subsystems would have to be added to the diagram to represent the buttons used to set up the new features (inputs) and the beeper (output).

Figure 8 shows three photos of the scales' display, each illustrating a different use. The top figure shows the display giving a reading in ounces; note that it displays fractions of an ounce. The middle figure shows the clock display; note that a colon is used in addition to the standard set of digits from 0 to 9. The bottom figure shows a weight displayed as a negative value. It may seem strange to have a 'negative weight', but it can occur when the add-and-weigh facility is used. Imagine that some ingredients are placed on the scalepan and the display reads 49 g. The user then invokes the add-and-weigh facility, so the display changes to 0 g. If the ingredients are then removed from the pan the display will read −49 g.

To implement these additional features the scales' computer has to represent all the additional data that could be output on the display by predetermined codes consisting of 1s and 0s. It has to represent fractional

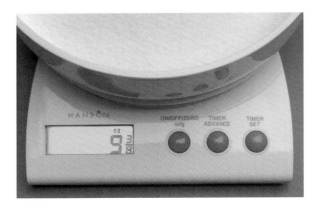

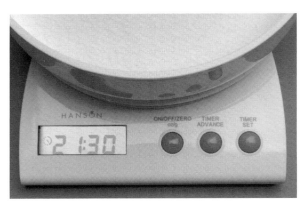

Figure 8   Three photos of the kitchen scales' display: (top) with the scales weighing in imperial units; (middle) with the timer function in operation; (bottom) negative values can be displayed for weights if the add-and-weigh facility is being used

data, negative numbers, a digital clock format and patterns to illuminate 'lb' and 'oz' as well as 'g'.

5.3   Digital camera

The last computer I am going to look at is the embedded computer in a digital camera.

Figure 9 shows a picture of a digital camera. The screen of the camera is displaying a picture that has previously been stored in a memory card within the camera. This memory card is not the camera computer's main memory, nor is it the secondary memory used to hold the computer's program; it is a form of removable secondary memory where the computer stores the images taken. Next to the camera in Figure 9 is an example of the memory card that this particular camera uses to store its images. The memory card can be unplugged from the camera and another memory card inserted.

Figure 9 Digital camera displaying image; a memory card is shown alongside

When the user presses the button to take a picture with a digital camera, its shutter opens, and the lens system focuses light from the image being photographed onto a device called a charge-coupled device or CCD. The CCD consists of a two-dimensional array of tiny light-sensitive cells that convert light into electrical charge. Figure 10 shows this array of cells and how the CCD is located behind the camera lens. The brighter the light that hits a cell, the greater the electrical charge that accumulates at that site. Once the camera shutter has closed, the information stored in the form of electrical charge at each cell is converted into a binary code and stored in the form of 1s and 0s in the camera's memory, and this forms the image captured by the camera. To collect colour information a system of colour filters is placed over the cells of the CCD. In Section 10.3 of this block you will look at this in more detail.

This stored raw data representing the image is then processed. The colour is reconstructed and adjusted, and techniques are used to sharpen the fine detail. The result of this process is a picture ready to be stored as a file in the camera's secondary memory. To reduce the amount of stored data, the file is usually compressed – that is, the number of bits used to represent the image is reduced. In some cameras the user can select options to choose the type of compression carried out. The process of compression is described later in this block.

Figure 11 shows the actions that the digital camera performs when taking a picture. Note that this diagram is not a functional block diagram of the camera but shows the actions that must occur to take and store the picture, in the order in which they must happen.

The digital camera shown in Figure 9 has some buttons that allow the user to set particular conditions when taking a picture. In addition to the button to take a picture, there are buttons to set the flash, control the preview of the stored images on the screen and set the zoom ratio. As there is a flash facility, there must also be a light-level meter incorporated into the camera; the level of light falling on the meter determines whether the flash will operate.

As with the PC and the electronic kitchen scales, a specific form of Figure 3 can be created for this digital camera.

Activity 9 (Exploratory)

Using the information about the digital camera given above, draw the specific form of Figure 3 for this camera.

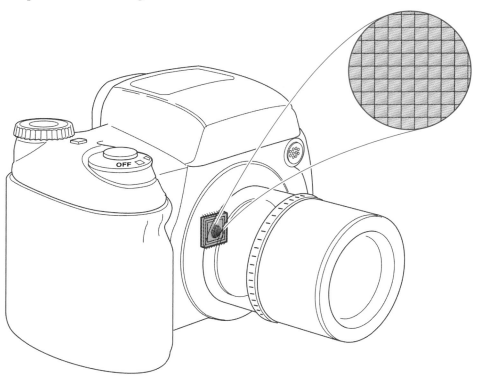

Figure 10   A representation of a CCD

Comment

This computer has main memory and also two items of secondary memory: the removable memory card and the internal secondary memory. The input devices are the CCD plus the buttons to take a picture, preview the stored images, set the flash and set the zoom ratio. The light meter is also an input device. The output devices are the camera's screen, the flash mechanism, the zoom and the control to open and shut the shutter. (If you are a camera enthusiast you may also have thought of the various controls for the shutter aperture, the focus etc., but as I have not explicitly mentioned them in the text I have not included them in my answer.)

Figure 12 shows all of this. Notice that this computer is complex, with a very wide range of input and output devices.

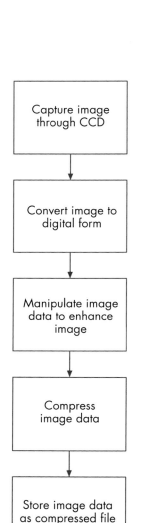

Figure 11   Diagram showing, in order, the processes that occur when taking a picture with a digital camera

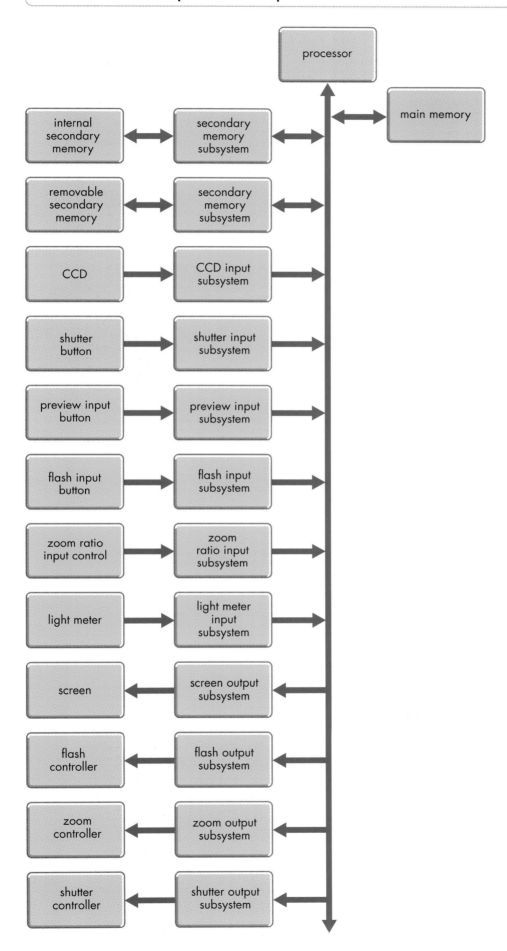

Figure 12   Functional block diagram for the digital camera

Normally the images stored in the camera are downloaded to a PC for viewing on the monitor and printing. One way of doing this is to take the memory card from the camera and put it into a memory card reader connected to the PC. If this is done, the memory card shifts from being a secondary memory of the camera to a secondary memory of the PC.

Another way of downloading the images is to use a USB cable, supplied with the camera, to connect the camera directly to the PC for data transfer.

5.4 Conclusion

You have seen that although the three products you have looked at are very different types of computer, they all embody the same basic functionality and a version of Figure 3 can be drawn for each product to illustrate this.

One feature of the PC is the range of forms of secondary memory it can use, and also the variety of input and output devices which the user can choose. The kitchen scales' embedded computer is relatively simple with no secondary memory and relatively few input and output devices. The computer within the camera has a processor which needs to implement several complex processes to manipulate the image, has secondary memory and has many input and output devices.

6 **A look to the future**

So what will computers do for you next? Perhaps they will be the key to solving transport problems. Driverless cars, controlled by computers, are under development. If these ever come to fruition perhaps they could help to reduce the number of road traffic accidents by automatically reducing their speed when they come too close to another car. Or perhaps journeys could be made faster and less frustrating because cars will use communicating computers to analyse traffic density and move along the road system without meeting traffic jams.

There is currently a system called the CIVIS bus that is being used in several European cities. It is not a driverless system, but the driver only controls the braking and not the steering for the bus. The bus uses an optical guidance system that follows a line on the road to keep the bus in a dedicated lane. The main advantage of this system over a conventional bus is the speed with which it can pull into and out of its bus stops. It is still far from the goal of a driverless system, but shows the progress being made.

You might find it attractive to buy a central-heating controller that could be accessed by a mobile phone to switch the heating on and off. Systems like this are becoming a reality, and the 'communicating house' or 'smart home' is predicted to be one of the great developments of the future. Perhaps in your home of the future the fridge will detect what food it contains and order items it knows (or believes) you are likely to need; sensors will detect levels of light and control the lighting and shut and open the curtains; and the heating will be controlled taking account of the number of people in the room.

It is obvious that as time goes on you are going to be surrounded by more and more systems that use computers. Even art is embracing this technology. Figure 13 describes a work of art that uses a camera and a processor to angle small reflective squares; as the squares tilt the effects generated change, making it a 'living' work.

Activity 10 (Exploratory)

Read the article given in Figure 13. Don't worry if, as is likely, you don't understand all the technical detail. What you have learnt from studying the course so far should allow you to form some basic answers to the questions below.

(a) What is the input device for this computer?

(b) What effect do the actions of the output devices create?

(c) A tile can take up to one of 255 positions to form the various shades of grey in the image. How many bits are needed for the 255 items of data needed to represent each position?

Comment

(a) The input device is a video camera that is located in the Wooden Mirror's centre.

Wooden Mirror

DANIEL ROZIN

The *Wooden Mirror* is an impressive physical presence, over 2 meters tall and 1.5 meters wide. Move in front of it, and its surface of wooden tiles comes alive. The tiles tilt up and down, and the resulting pattern of light and shade creates an image of whatever is before the mirror. Movement is reflected instantly by the tiles in ripples of motion, accompanied by a rustling sound reminiscent of a stiff breeze in a forest. To enable the mirror to create real-time images, artist Daniel Rozin connected a small video-camera in the mirror's center to a Macintosh computer. The image seen by the camera is digitized by the computer and reduced to a 35-by-29-pixel image with an 8-bit grayscale. The computer analyzes the differences between the current image and the previous frame and sends commands only to those tiles that need to be changed, using software written by Rozin. The tiles are tilted by a total of 830 servomotors, one per tile [bottom left], connected to a series of microcontrollers that are linked by serial lines to the Macintosh. Each tile can take up one of 255 positions to form the image, although in regular lighting conditions typically only 10 or 12 levels of gray can be discerned. Depending on how much activity it is mimicking, the mirror can refresh between 5 and 10 times a second.

"In many ways, this is the essence of what we try to do here: taking the power of digital computation and concealing it to see how it influences something more in touch with the human condition. Wood doesn't want to be very digital, each tile is slightly different. But computation can take all this randomness and messiness and put it into an order....The piece is on the line between analog and physical vs. digital and computational," explained creator Rozin, shown sitting in front of his creation [above left].

Rozin also strove to eliminate the concept of an interface. An interface "means putting some sort of membrane between you and the experience. With this, you understand immediately that it's a mirror, you know how to operate it, and no interface is involved."

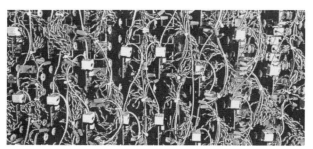

Figure 13   Art uses technology

(b) The output devices tilt the reflective tiles. The angle the tiles are tilted to causes a representation of the image seen by the video camera to be shown on the 'mirror'.

(c) Eight bits are needed as they can represent up to 256 different data items. Note that this ties in with a statement made in the article about how the computer reduces the camera image to an '8-bit grayscale'.

7 Computer programs

Earlier on I indicated that in order for a processor to perform a defined function it needs to be supplied with a list of instructions called a program. In this section I shall explore this idea a little further.

Software can be split into two categories, application software and operating systems. **Application software** is the name given to programs which enable a computer to perform specific tasks. The program that processes the image in the digital camera is one example; a word processor running on a PC is another.

application software

In computers that are running several application programs, the programs may well be sharing some of the computer's resources, such as its display or its hard disk. If this is the case then an **operating system** provides general-purpose software that controls the sharing of resources amongst the various programs, making sure that they are not competing for the same resource. The operating system on a PC makes it possible for, say, information about incoming e-mail to appear on the screen whilst a word processor is running and a document is printing. The operating system you are most likely to be familiar with is *Windows*®; the computing requirements for this course specify that you must have access to a PC running a *Windows*® operating system.

operating system

Very simple computers, such as the one in the kitchen scales, have only one program running and consist of a modest set of resources. In such simple systems the distinction between the operating system and the application program is not clearly defined, and it is not customary to distinguish between them. But in more complex computers an operating system becomes useful, and in something as complex as a PC it is a crucial component.

In Section 7.1 I will look a little more closely at operating systems. Then in Section 7.2 I will look at how application programs are developed.

7.1 Operating systems

You have already seen that operating systems organise the sharing of resources. But they do much more than this; they ensure the efficient running of a computer by:

- loading application programs from secondary memory into main memory and managing their execution;
- supporting application programs by managing their use of the computer's resources;
- managing the storage of programs and data in secondary memory;
- accepting inputs from and supplying outputs to the user.

In the next four paragraphs I'll examine each of these four aspects of an operating system in turn, using the PC as an example.

Unless an application program has been recently used and hence is already stored in main memory, the operating system will need to find the program in secondary memory, transfer it into main memory and arrange for the processor to execute it. If the user is running more than one application program, say a word processor and a drawing package, the operating system will need to manage execution of both in order to ensure that these two programs do not interfere with each other. When the user closes down an application program, the operating system has to manage this process and ensure that the computer can continue to operate normally.

Application programs make use of the computer's resources. For example, they send data to the display. Rather than the application program containing the instructions to perform tasks like this, they call on the operating system to perform the tasks on their behalf. This makes application programs easier to write.

In addition to organising the transfer of application programs from the secondary memory to the main memory, the operating system has to manage the process of storing application programs in secondary memory when the user first installs them. It also has to organise the storage of files that users create while they are running application programs. For example, with a word processor the operating system organises saving a newly created file to a folder specified by the user. On request, it also organises the retrieval of a previously saved file. Less obvious is the equally important task of storing and organising the temporary data generated by the word processor while it is running.

Accepting inputs from the user and generating outputs for the user are important functions of the operating system, and ones that can make a difference between a computer being easy to use or difficult. In the early days of PCs, users had to type text commands in order to get their computers to perform tasks, and all information from the computer came in the form of text. This was because the operating system of those days, DOS, did not have the 'graphical user interface' that everyone takes for granted today. There were no icons or menus on the screen, and pointing and clicking with a mouse was not an option. To a very large extent, it is the operating system, rather than the hardware, of a PC that influences how easy users find it to use.

In brief, the operating system in a PC not only controls the PC's resources but also hides many of the complexities of using a computer from the user, making the user's task easier.

I have taken the PC's operating system as an example, but the operating systems in those 'invisible' computers that have them should again hide the complexities of the computer from the user as well as control the sharing of resources.

You will learn more about operating systems in Block 4.

7.2 Using flowcharts to describe a task

Application programs are designed to perform specific tasks. These tasks range from the relatively simple to the extremely complex. In this section you will look at what is involved in planning a program to perform some simple tasks.

In order to write a program, the task the program will perform has to be first written as a list of actions. The actions have to be given in an order that will ensure the task is carried out successfully.

Activity 11 (Exploratory)

Write down, in order, the list of actions you would have to carry out to boil some water in an electric kettle.

Comment

The list of actions I would use to do this is:

> take lid off kettle
>
> turn on tap
>
> fill kettle with water
>
> monitor water level and turn off tap when correct
>
> put lid on kettle
>
> plug kettle in
>
> switch on kettle.

Your list may be different from mine. For example you may pour the water into the spout without taking the lid off, or the method of supplying power to the kettle might not use a switch. This doesn't matter. What is important is that you can see how even a very simple task can be described as a series of actions, and that these actions must be given in a particular order for the task to be carried out successfully. In my answer, for example, it would be impossible to carry out the action to put the lid on the kettle if I hadn't taken it off earlier in the sequence of actions.

Consider a very simple set of electronic scales. These scales have an on/off switch, but no other input buttons, and a display to show the weight of the object in the scalepan in grams.

Activity 12 (Exploratory)

Write down, in order, the list of actions that the computer inside the scales has to carry out in order to show an object's weight on the display.

Comment

The computer has to:

> accept data from the sensor that measures the displacement of the scalepan;
>
> transform the data from the sensor into data for the display;
>
> send the display-formatted data to the display.

The list of actions in the comment to Activity 12 can be shown diagrammatically in a type of diagram called a **flowchart**. Figure 14 shows how I have written this simple sequence of actions as a flowchart.

flowchart

The shapes of the symbols used in flowcharts are significant. Flowcharts are a common language used to communicate processes and it is important to be consistent in their use. This flowchart uses three different symbols to show:

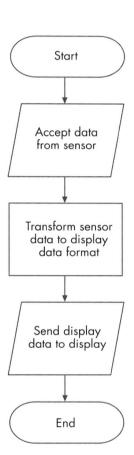

Figure 14 Flowchart of the tasks performed by simple electronic scales

- the start/end points of the process;
- data input or output;
- a process to be carried out.

Figure 15 defines these symbols. It also defines an additional symbol that shows a decision being made, and another for showing connectors.

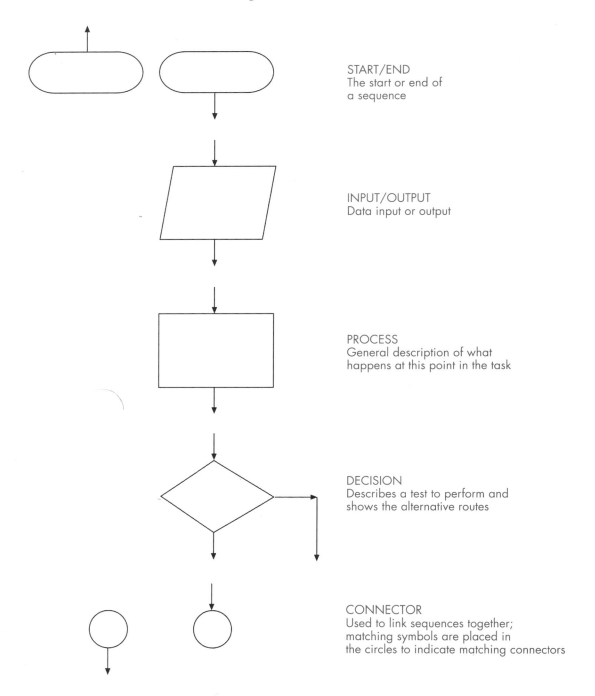

Figure 15 Flowchart symbols

In flowcharts, lines are used to connect symbols together, and arrows on these lines indicate the order in which tasks are carried out. You can see this in Figure 14.

My next example incorporates a decision box. It involves a slightly more complex set of electronic scales: they have one additional button on the front that allows the user to select whether the weight is displayed in grams or in pounds and ounces. A flowchart incorporating this choice of display format is shown in Figure 16. It uses the decision box to make a choice about which piece of the program will be run. There are two exit routes from the decision box; each route is called a **branch**. If the user has requested that the weight should be displayed in grams, the *Yes* branch is followed so that the sensor data can be transformed to gram format. If the user has requested that the weight should be displayed in pounds and ounces, the *No* branch is followed to transform the sensor data to pounds and ounces instead. Note that once the translation to the selected output format is complete the branches of the flowchart come together again and the 'send to display' part of the task is run regardless of which branch was taken earlier in the program.

branch

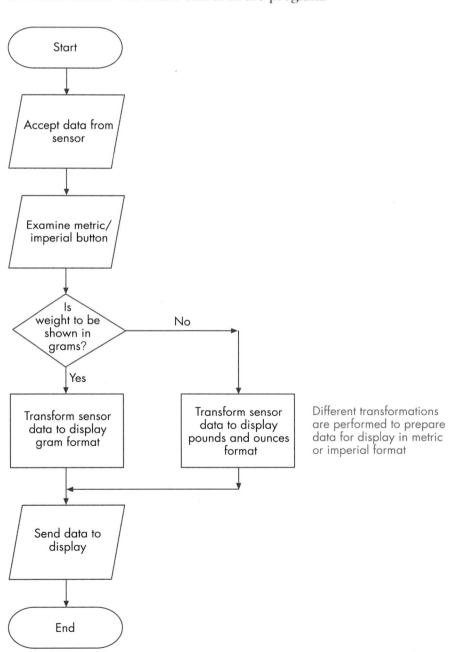

Figure 16   Flowchart for electronic scales with metric/imperial selector button

Now consider what happens when you are weighing, for example, flour on a set of scales. You slowly add more flour to the scalepan until you reach the desired weight. As you do this the display constantly changes, showing the weight increasing as you add more flour. To do this, the scales' computer must repeatedly examine the input and update the display each time it does so. The flowcharts in Figures 14 and 16 do not implement this. They simply take one reading and need to be re-started to take another.

loop

The flowchart can be changed so that the input is repeatedly examined and the output repeatedly displayed by means of what is called a **loop**. A loop allows a certain part of a flowchart to be carried out as many times as necessary depending on the results of a decision. In this instance, after every 'send to the display', the flowchart in Figure 17 shows a loop back to examine the sensor again, provided the scales have not been switched off. Note that a loop has to start as a branch from a decision box. Spend a few moments examining the loop in Figure 17; make sure that you understand how this flowchart differs from the one in Figure 16 and why it would enable the scales to display an increasing weight as, for example, flour was slowly added to the scalepan.

Activity 13 (Self assessment)

Figure 11 in Section 5 showed five boxes that form the basis for a flowchart describing the operation of a digital camera.

(a) You can now see that one of these boxes is in fact the wrong shape. Which box, and why?

(b) How can Figure 11 be expanded to show that the shutter has to be pressed before the image is captured? Draw the appropriate flowchart. It should incorporate a loop, start and end boxes and also two boxes with the text:

Examine shutter input

Is shutter pressed?

Comment

The answer is at the end of Block 1.

Activity 14 (Self assessment)

In Section 5 you met the idea that the user can switch the flash facility of the camera on or off, and that if the flash facility is switched on then a light reading will have to be taken and its value be used to determine if flash is needed. Draw a flowchart to describe this. The text for the boxes of your flowchart is given below, but not in the correct order. Where in the flowchart you drew for Activity 13 would your new flowchart fit?

Is light level above threshold?

Examine flash button input

Read light level

Prepare flash for use

Is flash input on?

Comment

The answer is at the end of Block 1.

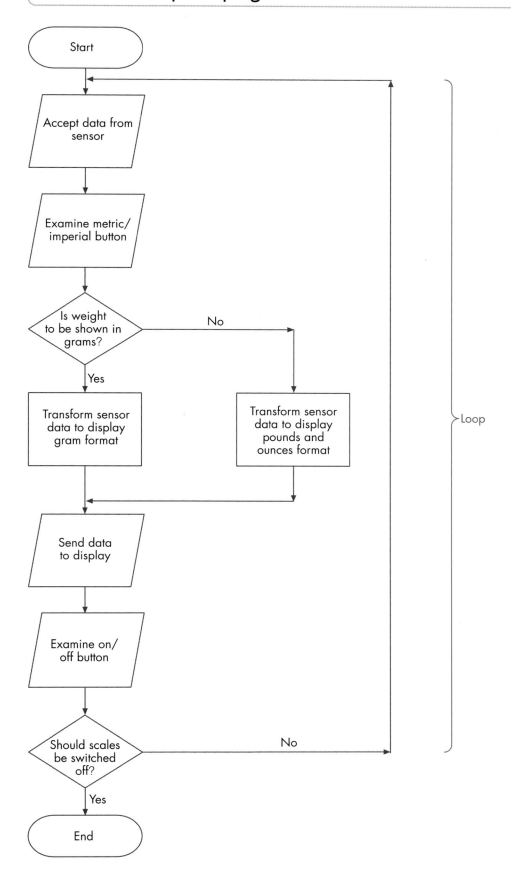

Figure 17   Flowchart for electronic scales incorporating a loop

Now here's an example of a task that an application program called a typing tutor needs to perform. A typing tutor checks how accurately the user types certain groups of letters at the computer keyboard. For example, the group 'asdf' might have to be typed ten times as follows 'asdf asdf asdf ...'. As the user types at the keyboard, the program checks that the correct letters have been typed in each group, using space characters to define where a group ends. When the program has counted that ten groups have been entered it displays how many correct and how many incorrect groups have been typed.

The flowchart to describe this task is rather complex, so you will work through it step by step. One helpful step would be to write down a list of actions in the same manner as you did for boiling the kettle.

Activity 15 (Exploratory)

Starting with the two actions given below, write, in order, the list of actions that need to be carried out to complete the task of the typing tutor.

> Read in a group of letters from the keyboard
>
> If the letters are asdf then count this as a good entry and ...

Comment

A suitable list of actions would be:

> Read in a group of letters from the keyboard
>
> If the letters are asdf then count this as a good entry and add 1 to the total of good entries
>
> If the letters are not asdf then count this as a bad entry and add 1 to the total of bad entries
>
> Add 1 to the number of groups received
>
> If 10 groups have been received then send the data about performance to the display
>
> If 10 groups have not been received then get another group of letters

Activity 16 (Self assessment)

Use the answer to Activity 15 to help you to produce a flowchart for implementing the task of the typing tutor. (Hint: you will not be able to use exactly the words shown above in some of the boxes of your flowchart. In particular, think carefully about how you will implement the sentences beginning with 'if' in the flowchart.)

Comment

The answer is at the end of Block 1.

You have now seen several examples of how flowcharts can be used to describe tasks carried out by computers. Drawing such flowcharts is just one stage in the process of developing an application program. The process of developing any software starts with an analysis of the task or tasks to be performed by the computer, an analysis designed to tease out just how the computer is to behave under every possible circumstance. The software development process may continue through the drawing of flowcharts like the ones you have just met, or the software developers may prefer other means of arriving at an understanding of each individual element of the task and how these elements fit together. In either case, however, the next step will be to write the computer program. This will take the various elements of the task and convert them into a program by use of a **programming language**, which is a structured language with a limited set of words and symbols and which can be used to tell a computer how to perform a task. Finally, the program must be 'debugged' (made free of errors) through extensive testing, and also documented to facilitate any future work on it. You will meet one very simple programming language in Block 2, when you work with the course's simulated processor, and you will get a small taste of the software development process.

programming language

Activity 17 (Review/Exam preparation)

Now is a good point for you to turn to your *Block 1 Companion* and look at the tables of learning outcomes. You will find that there are spaces in the middle column for you to write in the section or sections of Block 1 that enable you to fulfil the learning outcomes, and also spaces for you to write in an activity or activities that enable you to check you have fulfilled the outcome. I suggest that you fill in as many of these spaces as is appropriate for this stage of your study of Block 1. This will help you to monitor your progress through this first block, and will be helpful in the future when you come to revise for the exam.

8 Representing data in computers: introduction

You have seen from Section 2 of this block that a computer is designed to do the following things:

- *receive* data from the outside world;
- *store* that data;
- *manipulate* that data, probably creating and storing more data while doing so;
- *present* data back to the outside world.

In the next few sections I am going to examine in more detail the data that a computer receives, stores, manipulates and presents. In particular, I want to explore the idea that in a computer the data *represents* something in the outside world.

Here are a couple of examples you are probably familiar with from using your PC. The data will represent text and punctuation marks if you are using your PC to do word processing. The data will represent numbers if you are using your PC to do calculations on a spreadsheet. Many applications, not just word processors and spreadsheets, require the representation of text and/or numbers, but there are also other types of data that need to be represented.

Activity 18 (Exploratory)

Think back to the three examples of computers introduced earlier in this block: the kitchen scales, the digital camera and the PC. Use these examples to suggest what else will need to be represented in these computers. For instance, weights will need to be represented in the electronic kitchen scales, where they are an input.

Comment

You may have suggested the following:

> numbers on a display panel (outputs in the kitchen scales)
>
> sound produced by a beeper (output when the kitchen scales' timer facility is used)
>
> scenes that will be turned into still pictures (inputs in the digital camera)
>
> still pictures (outputs in the digital camera and in PCs)
>
> scenes that will be turned into moving pictures (inputs in PCs with web cams)
>
> moving pictures (outputs in PCs)
>
> music, spoken words and other types of sound (inputs and outputs in PCs).

Another, more subtle, input that you may have mentioned is the input from a button on the kitchen scales or digital camera. Think, for example, of the button on the digital camera that switches the flash on or off. A representation of the input from this button is an important data item in the camera's computer: it tells the computer whether flash is to be used.

Data is an important part of any computer system, and Sections 9 to 11 will discuss the ways in which various types of data can be represented in a computer, focusing on the three example computers from earlier in this block: the kitchen scales in Section 9, the digital camera in Section 10 and the PC in Section 11.

A danger with using specific examples to introduce a general idea like data representation is that the examples may not demonstrate all the principles that need to be introduced. I have dealt with this potential problem by inserting 'boxes' at various points in the text. These discuss ideas about data representation which are related to those in the main text but either are not relevant to the particular example under discussion, or apply more widely. You should note that the material in these boxes *is assessable*.

You have already met a working definition of 'data', back in Section 1. I now need to formalise that definition. The word 'data' itself is a Latin one and its root meaning is 'things given', hence 'facts'. But in the context of computers the word '**data**' has a subtly different meaning, which is *a formalised representation of facts, entities or ideas such that they can be manipulated, transmitted and/or received*. Note that this means that 'data' is therefore being given a different meaning from 'information'. Information is also facts and ideas, but not in a formalised representation. For use by a computer, information must be converted to, or expressed in, a suitable formalised format, and it is this formalised format which is called data.

data

You should also be aware from Section 4 of this block that in computers all data is represented as *binary codes*. That is, all data is represented as strings of 0s and 1s. You also need to recall that a single binary digit – that is, a 1 or a 0 – is called a *bit*, and that the term *byte* is used to refer to a group of eight bits.[4]

As with all codes, *the user must know what the coding convention is in order to be able to assign meaning to it*. For instance, on one occasion in a computer it may be appropriate to assign the meaning 'the letter J' to the code 01001010; on another occasion it may be appropriate to assign the meaning 'the number 74' to the same code, and so on. Does this sound faintly alarming? How does the computer 'know' whether to treat 01001010 as the letter J or the number 74 or something else? The answer is that context is crucial: if the computer has been programmed to treat the next code it receives as a letter, it will treat the code 01001010 as the letter J; if the computer has been programmed to treat the next code it receives as a number, then it will treat the code 01001010 as the number 74; and if it has been programmed to treat the next code it receives as something else, then it will treat the code 01001010 as that something else.

---

[4] 'Byte' is the term traditionally used for a group of 8 bits in the context of computers. But 'octet' is the term traditionally used for a group of 8 bits in the context of communications. Now that computers and communications are converging you may meet either term in either context. You therefore need to be familiar with both terms.

Inside a computer, the codes are grouped into pre-defined numbers of bits. Sometimes, particularly in relatively simple computers such as the kitchen scales, these pre-defined groups are bytes. But many computers are designed to handle a longer group of bits as a single entity. Modern PCs handle 32-bit groups, and it is likely that they will be handling 64-bit groups in the near future.

data word
word
word length

A fixed length group of bits that is handled in a computer as a single entity is called a **data word**, or simply a **word**, and the number of bits in the word is referred to as the **word length**. Thus most PCs work with a word length of 32 bits.

Representing data in the kitchen scales

> *Study note: You may like to have the T224 Numeracy Resource to hand as you study Section 9. It offers additional explanations and extra practice on some of the topics, and you may find this useful.*

The kitchen scales you met earlier in this block provide examples of several different types of data that need to be represented.

I'll start with an output: the display panel on the front of the scales. You saw that this could display numbers: integer (whole) numbers of grams; numbers of ounces including fractions; even negative numbers when the add-and-weigh facility is in use. In Sections 9.1 to 9.3 I shall discuss how integer numbers which are positive, fractions and negative numbers respectively can be represented inside the computer.

So far as the inputs to the computer are concerned, the most important one is the weight in the scalepan. You may think that representing a weight inside a computer is simply a matter of representing a number, and to some extent you would be right. But there is a complication, which I'll explain in Section 9.4.

Next I'll deal with the input that controls whether the scales are to weigh in metric or imperial units and the output that controls whether the beeper that's used in the timer function is on or off. Representing both of these needs a true/false quantity, as I'll explain in Section 9.5.

All of the above deal with the codes that are used to represent the data. I'll conclude Section 9 with a brief look (Section 9.6) at the ways in which input and output are handled so that the computer can obtain the data it uses, and subsequently present the user with appropriate data.

9.1 Representing numbers: positive integers

A very straightforward way of finding binary codes to represent positive integers is simply to use the binary number that corresponds to each integer. This is because every positive integer in the everyday number system (known as the decimal or denary system because it uses 10 different digits) has a corresponding number in the binary number system.

As you will see later, in Section 14 of this block, just as arithmetic (addition, subtraction, etc.) can be performed on everyday denary numbers, so it can also be performed on binary numbers. This means that encoding denary numbers as binary numbers is particularly useful whenever an application will include arithmetic. And this is the case with the kitchen scales, thanks to their add-and-weigh function.

You need to know something about binary numbers, and so in this section I shall first remind you of an important principle of the number system you are already familiar with, the 10-digit decimal or denary system, then show how that principle applies to the 2-digit binary number system. I'll also show you how to convert between the two systems.

9.1.1 Denary numbers

denary representation
decimal representation

The number system which we all use in everyday life is called the **denary representation**, or sometimes the **decimal representation**, of numbers. In this system, the ten digits 0 to 9 are used, either singly or in ordered groups. The important point for you to grasp is that when the digits are used in ordered groups, each digit is understood to have a

weighting

weighting. For example, consider the denary number 549. Here 5 has the weighting of hundreds, 4 has the weighting of tens and 9 has the weighting of units. (Try saying 549 aloud: five hundred and forty nine. If you remember that 'ty' is a corruption of 'ten' you can see that the way the number is said is exactly consistent with this idea of weightings.)

$$\left.\begin{array}{ccc} 10^2 & 10^1 & 10^0 \\ \text{hundred} & \text{ten} & \text{unit} \end{array}\right\} \text{weightings}$$
$$\begin{array}{ccc} 5 & 4 & 9 \end{array}$$

So 549 stands for:

$$(5 \times 10^2) + (4 \times 10^1) + (9 \times 10^0)$$

which is:

$$(5 \times 100) + (4 \times 10) + (9 \times 1)$$

exponent

In the foregoing, the raised numbers after the various tens are called **exponents**. If you are unfamiliar with exponent notation, you should note that 10^2 means 10×10, 10^3 means $10 \times 10 \times 10$, and so on. 10^1 simply means 10 and 10^0 is taken to be 1. There is more about this in the T224 Numeracy Resource if it's an unfamiliar idea to you.

The position of the digit in the group is therefore crucial in determining its weighting. The leftmost digit in the group (5 in the above example) is called the most-significant digit because it is the most heavily weighted digit. Similarly, the rightmost digit (9 above) is called the least-significant digit.

positional notation

A number representation like this, where a digit's position determines its weighting, is called a **positional notation**. Notice the pattern of the exponents; they increase by 1 from right to left.

Activity 19 (Self assessment)

In the denary number 10 276:

(a) What are the weightings of

　　(i)　the 7

　　(ii)　the 0

　　(iii)　the 1?

(b) What is the most-significant digit?

(c) Write out this number in a similar way to the way 549 was written out in the preceding text – that is, as a sum of terms of the form (digit × 10 to some exponent).

Comment

The answer is at the end of Block 1.

9.1.2 Binary numbers

Just as a denary number system uses ten different digits (0, 1, 2, 3, ... 9), a **binary number** system uses two (0, 1).

Once again the idea of positional notation is important. You have just seen that the weightings which apply to the digits in a denary number are the exponents of *ten*. With binary numbers, where only two digits are used, the weightings applied to the digits are exponents of *two*.

The rightmost bit is given the weighting of 2^0, which is 1. The next bit to the left is given a weighting of 2^1, which is 2, and so on.

Thus the 4-bit binary number 1101 represents:

2^3	2^2	2^1	2^0	
eight	four	two	one	} weightings
1	1	0	1	

The leftmost bit is called the **most-significant bit (m.s.b.)** and the rightmost bit is called the **least-significant bit (l.s.b.)**.

Computers are designed to work with binary numbers, but denary numbers suit most people better. Humans therefore need to interpret the 4-bit binary number 1101 as follows:

$$(1 \times 2^3) + (1 \times 2^2) + (0 \times 2^1) + (1 \times 2^0)$$

which is $8 + 4 + 0 + 1 = 13$ in denary.

Activity 20 (Self assessment)

What does the 4-bit binary number 1010 represent? To what denary number is it equal? What is its most-significant bit?

Comment

The answer is at the end of Block 1.

Exactly the same principles can be applied to larger binary numbers. For example, in an 8-bit word the most-significant bit has a weighting of 2^7, which is 128. So 10110110 represents:

2^7	2^6	2^5	2^4	2^3	2^2	2^1	2^0	
(128)	(64)	(32)	(16)	(8)	(4)	(2)	(1)	} weightings
1	0	1	1	0	1	1	0	

and equals $128 + 0 + 32 + 16 + 0 + 4 + 2 + 0$, which is 182 in denary.

It is often convenient to number the bits in a binary word and to refer to the bits as 'bit 5' or 'bit 2'. And the most convenient way of numbering

binary number

**most-significant bit
m.s.b.
least-significant bit
l.s.b.**

the bits is to use the exponents in the weightings. So the bits are usually numbered as follows (for an 8-bit word):

7	6	5	4	3	2	1	0	bit number
2^7	2^6	2^5	2^4	2^3	2^2	2^1	2^0	weighting

This scheme means that the least-significant bit is bit 0 and the most-significant bit is bit 7.

Just as a space between groups of three digits in large numbers (e.g. 625 127) can make them easier to read, so spaces between groups of four bits can make binary numbers easier to read. I shall use spaces in this way. So I shall write, for example, 1001 1110 rather than 10011110. Note that the space is purely for convenience in reading the number; it does not affect the value of the number in any way, nor the way the computer handles it.

Activity 21 (Self assessment)

(a) To what denary number is the binary number 1100 0110 equal?

(b) In a 16-bit word, what is the weighting of the most-significant bit? What bit number should be allocated to this bit?

(c) To what denary number is the binary number 1000 0000 0000 0001 equal?

Note that Windows has a calculator (in Accessories) that will evaluate numbers like 2^{10}, 2^{14}, etc. You will need to choose Scientific from its View menu and then use the x^y key. For instance, to find 2^{10} press 2 then x^y then 10 then = . You should get 1024.

Comment

The answer is at the end of Block 1.

Counting in binary is very simple because there are only two possible digits. It proceeds as follows:

```
   0
   1
  10
  11
 100
 101
 110
 111
1000
 etc.
```

Notice that when all the bits in any number are 1, the next higher number needs one more bit to represent it. This is exactly analogous to denary, where 999 is followed by 1000, which needs one more digit to represent it.

Activity 22 (Self assessment)

(a) What binary number follows

    (i) 1 1111

    (ii) 1 0111?

(b) What binary number precedes 1000 0000?

Comment

The answer is at the end of Block 1.

9.1.3 Converting denary numbers to binary

If computers encode the denary numbers of the everyday world as binary numbers, then clearly there needs to be conversion from denary to binary and vice versa. You have just seen how to convert binary numbers to denary, because I did a couple of examples to show you how binary numbers 'work'. But how can denary numbers be converted to binary? I'll show you by means of an example.

Example 1

Convert 219 to an 8-bit binary number.

Answer

First write out the weightings of an 8-bit number:

2^7	2^6	2^5	2^4	2^3	2^2	2^1	2^0
(128)	(64)	(32)	(16)	(8)	(4)	(2)	(1)

Now decide whether the given number, 219, is larger than or equal to the largest weighting, 128. If the given number is larger than or equal to the weighting, record a 1 in the '128' column and subtract the weighting from the number. But if the given number is smaller than the weighting, record a 0 in the '128' column.

Here 219 is bigger than 128. Hence a 1 goes into the '128' column (there is one '128' in 219). This is shown below. The result of the subtraction 219 − 128 is 91.

2^7	2^6	2^5	2^4	2^3	2^2	2^1	2^0
(128)	(64)	(32)	(16)	(8)	(4)	(2)	(1)
1							

Now decide whether the result of the subtraction, 91, is larger than or equal to than the next-lower weighting, 64. (I'll just call the result of the subtraction 'the new number'.) If the new number is larger than or equal to the weighting, record a 1 in the '64' column and subtract the weighting from the new number. If the new number is smaller than the weighting, record a 0 in the '64' column.

Here 91 is larger than 64. Hence a 1 goes into the '64' column (there is one '64' in 91). This is shown below. The result of the subtraction 91 − 64 is 27.

2^7	2^6	2^5	2^4	2^3	2^2	2^1	2^0
(128)	(64)	(32)	(16)	(8)	(4)	(2)	(1)
1	1						

Now decide whether the new number, 27, is larger than or equal to the next-lower weighting, 32. If the new number is larger than or equal to the weighting, record a 1 in the '32' column and subtract the weighting from the new number. If the new number is smaller than the weighting, record a 0 in the '32' column.

Here 27 is smaller than 32. Hence a 0 goes into the '32' column (there are no '32s' in 27):

2^7	2^6	2^5	2^4	2^3	2^2	2^1	2^0
(128)	(64)	(32)	(16)	(8)	(4)	(2)	(1)
1	1	0					

Now decide whether the number brought forward, 27, is larger than or equal to the next-lower weighting, 16. If the number brought forward is larger than or equal to the weighting, record a 1 in the '16' column and subtract the weighting from the new number. If the number brought forward is smaller than the weighting, record a 0 in the '16' column.

Here 27 is larger than 16. Hence a 1 goes into the '16' column (there is one '16' in 27). This is shown below. The result of the subtraction 27 – 16 is 11.

2^7	2^6	2^5	2^4	2^3	2^2	2^1	2^0
(128)	(64)	(32)	(16)	(8)	(4)	(2)	(1)
1	1	0	1				

The process continues for the last four remaining weightings, and you can check for yourself that the final result is:

2^7	2^6	2^5	2^4	2^3	2^2	2^1	2^0
(128)	(64)	(32)	(16)	(8)	(4)	(2)	(1)
1	1	0	1	1	0	1	1

The binary number can now be read off; it is 1101 1011.

Sometimes the first bit, or the first few bits, turn out to be 0 – as would be the case if, say, denary 6 was being converted to an 8-bit number. These 'leading zeros' must be included in the resulting binary number, otherwise it would not be 8 bits long. So, for example, 6 is 0000 0110 in 8-bit representation.

The same principles as those illustrated in the example above apply to other word lengths; the important point is to start the comparison-and-subtraction process with the weighting of the most-significant bit for the word length you are using.

Activity 23 (Self assessment)

(a) Convert denary 7 into a 4-bit number.

(b) Convert the following denary numbers into 8-bit numbers:

   (i) 120   (ii) 13

Comment

The answer is at the end of Block 1.

Activity 24 (Exploratory)

Is there more than one possible result of converting a denary number into a binary number? Look back at the conversion of 219 (my example) and of 7, 120 and 13 (Activity 23) to help you to decide.

Comment

There is only one possible pattern of 1s and 0s in binary that equals a given denary number. You can alter things slightly by saying whether you want a 4-bit, 8-bit, 16-bit, etc. word (for example denary 7 is 0111 in a 4-bit word, but 0000 0111 in an 8-bit word), but the essence of the pattern stays the same.

This is because there is only one possible outcome of the comparison at each stage of the conversion process: either the number you are working with is larger than or equal to the next weighting or it is smaller than the next weighting. There is no possible ambiguity. Hence the pattern of 1s and 0s is fully defined and only one appropriate pattern can exist.

In conclusion, then, if the denary number to be encoded is a positive integer (a positive whole number), then the number is converted to binary form, as just described, so that it can be stored or manipulated in the computer. And after manipulation the result can be converted back to denary for reporting the outcome to the user. In the kitchen scales, for example, the weight is displayed as a denary number on the display.

Distinguishing between binary and denary numbers

Very often it's obvious whether a given number is binary or denary: 2975 is denary, and 0011 1010 is very likely (though not absolutely certain) to be binary. But is the number 1001 binary or denary?

One way of distinguishing clearly between binary and denary numbers is to write a subscript 2 at the end of a binary number and a subscript 10 at the end of a denary number. Thus

   1001_2

is binary because of the subscript 2 at the end, whereas

   1001_{10}

is denary because of the subscript 10 at the end.

Sometimes binary numbers are described as being 'to base 2'. This fits with the subscript 2 at the end of the number. Similarly, denary numbers can be described as being 'to base 10', and this fits with the subscript 10 at the end.

You will meet the subscript convention on occasions in the rest of the course.

9.1.4   Encoding larger integers

The examples and activities in this section have looked only at 8-bit numbers. They have illustrated all of the principles of encoding positive integers as binary numbers without introducing the complication of larger numbers. But of course with 8 bits only relatively small integers can be encoded.

Activity 25 (Self assessment)

What is the largest positive integer that can be encoded using just 8 bits?

Comment

The answer is at the end of Block 1.

You may remember from Section 4 that there is a pattern to how many different integers can be encoded by a given number of bits. You have just seen in Activity 25 that with 8 bits (one byte) only the denary integers 0 to 255 can be encoded. This is 256 different integers in all. So 8 bits can encode 256 different integers, and 256 is 2^8. If you check, you will find that with 4 bits 2^4 (16) different integers can be encoded, with 6 bits, 2^6 (64) different integers. This leads to the general rule that with n bits 2^n different integers can be encoded.

Using this general rule, 16 bits can encode 2^{16} different positive integers, which is 65 536. So the denary integers 0 to 65 535 can be encoded in 16 bits, which is 2 bytes. Similarly 32 bits can encode 2^{32} different positive integers, which is 4 294 967 296. So the denary integers 0 to 4 294 967 295 can be represented in 32 bits, which is 4 bytes.

Activity 26 (Exploratory)

Did you notice that I said that with 2 bytes 65 536 different positive integers can be encoded, and then that they are 0 to 65 535? Why did I not say that they are 0 to 65 536?

Comment

In this method of encoding, a code of all zeros always represents denary 0. This leaves only 65 536 − 1 = 65 535 other patterns of 0s and 1s to represent other integers. So only the 65 535 integers 1 to 65 535 can be represented along with the 0.

The kitchen scales have been designed so that when they are weighing in metric they can weigh up to 3000 grams, in whole numbers of grams. I'm going to ignore for the moment the fact that the kitchen scales can handle both positive and negative integers, which is an added complication that I shall come to in Section 9.3. Imagine that the scales did not have the add-and-weigh facility and so did not need to deal with negative numbers. Then they would simply need to be able to encode positive integers from 0 to 3000.

Activity 27 (Exploratory)

How many bits are needed to encode positive integers from 0 to 3000? Hint: you already know that 8 bits would offer too few codes ($2^8 = 256$) and 16 too many ($2^{16} = 65\,536$). So try some numbers between 8 and 16.

Comment

Eleven bits would offer 2048 different codes, which is too few. Twelve bits offer 4096, which is more than enough. So 12 bits are needed to encode positive integers from 0 to 3000.

Now it so happens that the computer in the kitchen scales uses 8-bit words. So how could it cope with the fact that 12 bits are needed to hold the codes for the weights in grams? The answer is very simple: two words would be used. One word would hold the rightmost 8 bits of the code, the other word the leftmost 4 (with some spare bits that are not used.) Figure 18 illustrates this for the code 0101 0111 1100. Note that the word on the left in Figure 18 is the most significant, as it holds the most-significant bits of the code word. The one on the right is the least significant.

not used

0101   01111100

most-significant word   least-significant word

Figure 18   The 12-bit code word 0101 0111 1100 is held in two 8-bit data words

Provided the program had been carefully designed to take account of this arrangement, everything would work just fine.

A representation that uses more than one word is known as a **multiple-length representation**.

multiple-length representation

Activity 28 (Self assessment)

Read the box 'Binary-coded decimal' to help you to answer this question.

What is the denary equivalent of the binary word

     0101 0110

if it represents

(a) a natural binary number

(b) a binary-coded decimal number with two code words packed into the single 8-bit word?

Comment

The answer is at the end of Block 1.

natural binary

binary-coded decimal
BCD

> ### Binary-coded decimal
>
> The coding system described in Section 9.1 is known as the **natural binary** coding system. It uses the binary counting numbers 0, 1, 10, 11, 100, etc. to encode the denary counting numbers 0, 1, 2, 3, 4, etc.
>
> There is an alternative coding system which is sometimes used. It is known as **binary-coded decimal** or **BCD**. Here each digit of a denary number is coded by its 4-bit binary equivalent. This results in as many 4-bit code words as there are digits in the original denary number. So for example denary 25 is encoded as:
>
> 0010 (two) then 0101 (five)
>
> and denary 139 as:
>
> 0001 (one) then 0011 (three) then 1001 (nine).
>
> In a computer with, say, a 16-bit word length, four BCD code words can be packed into a single computer word if desired. Alternatively, each code word can form the least-significant four bits of a 16-bit word, with the other bits set to 0. It is important to make a decision on this point in each individual application, and then adhere to it.

9.2 Representing numbers: fractions

In the denary system, a decimal point can be used to represent fractions, as in 6.5 or 24.29. One way of encoding fractions uses an exactly analogous method in binary numbers: a 'binary point' is inserted.

Some examples of 8-bit binary fractions are:

    0.0010110

    110.01101

    0101110.1

The weightings that are applied to the bits after the binary point are, reading from left to right, 1/2, 1/4, 1/8, etc. (in just the same way as in denary fractions they are 1/10, 1/100, etc.).

Now, 1/4 is the same as $1/2^2$, and 1/8 is the same as $1/2^3$, and there is a convenient notation for fractions like this, which is to write $1/2^2$ as 2^{-2}, $1/2^3$ as 2^{-3}, and so on. In other words, a negative sign in the exponent indicates a fraction.

Using this notation, the bits after the binary point in a binary fraction are weighted as follows:

2^{-1}	2^{-2}	2^{-3}	2^{-4}	...
(1/2 = 0.5)	(1/4 = 0.25)	(1/8 = 0.125)	(1/16 = 0.0625)	...

So, for instance, 0.010 1000 in binary is equal to 1/4 + 1/16 = 5/16 (or 0.25 + 0.0625 = 0.3125) in denary.

One problem with encoding fractions like this is that there is no obvious way of representing the binary point itself within a computer word. Given the 8-bit number 0101 1001, where should the point lie? The way of solving this problem is to adopt a convention that, throughout a particular application, the binary point will be taken to lie between two specified bits. This is called the **fixed-point representation**. Once a convention has been adopted – for example, that the binary point lies between bits 7 and 6 – it should be adhered to throughout the application.

fixed-point representation

Another problem is that it may not be possible to represent a denary fraction *exactly* with a word of given length. For example, it is not possible to represent denary 0.1 exactly with an 8-bit word. The nearest to it is binary 0.000 1101 with a denary difference of 0.0015625. (Try it for yourself!) So it is just not possible to represent all fractions exactly with a binary word of fixed length. This second problem can be reduced, but not eliminated, if a multiple-length representation is used. For example, with 12 bits the denary fraction still cannot be represented exactly, but now the nearest to it is binary 0.000 1100 1101 with a much smaller denary difference of 0.00009765625.

Fortunately this problem of exact representation does not occur in the kitchen-scales example. In recipes using imperial weights it is traditional to use 1/2 oz, 1/4 oz, etc., and these are fractions which can be exactly represented by the fixed-point representation just described.

Floating-point representation

Another way of representing binary fractions is by the **floating-point representation**. This is the preferred method in many applications as it is a very flexible method, though rather complex. It uses the same basic idea as a fixed-point fraction, but with a variable scale factor. Two groups of bits are used to represent a single quantity. The first group, called the **mantissa**, contains the value of a fixed-point binary fraction with the binary point in some predefined position – say, after the most-significant bit. The second group, called the **exponent**, contains an integer that is the scale factor.

floating-point representation

mantissa

exponent

An example is a mantissa of 0.111 1000, which evaluates to the fixed-point fraction $1/2 + 1/4 + 1/8 + 1/16 = 15/16$, together with an exponent of 0000 0011, which evaluates to the denary integer 3. But what fraction does this mantissa–exponent pair represent?

The answer is that it represents (mantissa $\times\ 2^{\text{exponent}}$), which is $15/16 \times 2^3$. This works out to $15/16 \times 8$, which is 7.5.

Another example is a mantissa of 0.011 0000 and an exponent of 0000 0001. Here the mantissa evaluates to $1/4 + 1/8$, which is 3/8. The exponent evaluates to 1. So the fraction represented here is $3/8 \times 2^1$. This works out to $3/8 \times 2$, which is 3/4.

Notice that the fraction being represented in the first example is a 'mixed fraction' – that is, a mixture of an integer and a fraction which is less than 1 – while in the second example the fraction being represented is simply less than 1. This ability to represent both types of fractions with identical encoding methods makes the floating-point representation extremely versatile.

9.3 Representing numbers: negative integers

In Section 9.1 I showed you how integers can be encoded if they are known to be positive, treating the integers in the kitchen scales as if they were known to be positive. However, if the user invokes the 'add-and-weigh' function on the scales while there is an object in the scalepan and then removes the object, the display should record a negative value. Hence the computer in the scales must be able to carry out subtractions and deal with resulting negative values. If the user is moving several things on and off the scalepan, invoking the 'add-and-weigh' function on occasions, then the computer must be able to determine at all times what value it is to display and whether this value is positive or negative. The computer must, therefore, be able (a) to do arithmetic, (b) to handle negative values and (c) to distinguish between positive and negative values.

In this section I shall show you how negative numbers can be encoded and distinguished from positive numbers. The aspect of arithmetic will be dealt with later, in Section 14.

signed integer

An integer which may be positive or negative is known as a **signed integer**. In any code system for signed integers, it is important to indicate whether the integer is positive or negative.

additive inverse

With ordinary denary numbers, a signed positive integer is prefixed by a plus sign and a signed negative integer is prefixed by a minus sign. Each signed integer has an **additive inverse** which is obtained by replacing the plus sign by a minus sign, or vice versa. For example, $+5$ has the additive inverse -5; -20 has the additive inverse $+20$, and so on. A number and its additive inverse have the property that zero is obtained when they are added together. This system of representation is called the **sign-and-magnitude system**.

sign-and-magnitude system

You will probably be very familiar with the sign-and-magnitude system, and it is tempting to try to find a way of using it for binary numbers, perhaps by making the most-significant bit into a 'sign bit' and saying that 0000 0101 is $+5$ while 1000 0101 is -5. Unfortunately, however, this coding system would make arithmetic with binary numbers awkward for computers and so it is not normally used.

The coding system that is used adapts the positional notation I introduced in Section 9.1 to allow for negative numbers. Specifically, the most-significant bit is given a *negative* weighting. With 8-bit codes, the weightings are then as follows:

7	6	5	4	3	2	1	0	bit number
-2^7	2^6	2^5	2^4	2^3	2^2	2^1	2^0	
(-128)	(64)	(32)	(16)	(8)	(4)	(2)	(1)	weightings

The advantage of this system is that it makes the addition and subtraction of signed integers more straightforward for the computer's processor, as you'll see in Section 14.

Example 2

Convert the signed binary integer 1101 0110 to denary.

Answer

Using the weightings for 8-bit signed integers, 1101 0110 is equivalent to:

-2^7	2^6	2^5	2^4	2^3	2^2	2^1	2^0
(-128)	(64)	(32)	(16)	(8)	(4)	(2)	(1)
1	1	0	1	0	1	1	0

which is $-128 + 64 + 16 + 4 + 2 = -42$ in denary.

In this coding system, the leftmost bit (bit 7) is 0 for a positive number and 1 for a negative number, so at first glance you might think of it simply as a 'sign bit'. But this leftmost bit does more than simply acting as a 'sign bit': it contributes -128 to the number whenever its value is 1, thereby forcing the number to be negative whenever it is 1.

This system of encoding is called the **2's complement system** and the resulting codes are often referred to as **2's complement numbers**.

2's complement system
2's complement numbers

The process of converting a *positive* denary 8-bit number to its 2's complement equivalent is almost identical to the process of converting a denary number to an ordinary binary number. As it is positive, it cannot have a *minus* 128 in it, and so the leftmost bit is 0. The conversion process then starts by comparing the largest *positive* power of 2 with the given number.

If a *negative* denary number is to be converted, however, it must first be expressed as the sum of a negative and a positive number, as the following example shows.

Example 3

Convert the denary number -122 to an 8-bit 2's complement number.

Answer

The sign bit of an 8-bit 2's complement number has weighting -128. Therefore -122 must be expressed as:

$$-128 + \text{(a positive number)}$$

Clearly here the appropriate positive number is 6, so -122 is $-128 + 6$.

Because the number contains -128, the leftmost bit of the binary representation is 1. The other 7 bits are the 7-bit binary equivalent of 6, which is 000 0110. So the 8-bit 2's complement equivalent of -122 is:

1000 0110.

The rule is first to add 128 to the negative number, then to convert the result to a 7-bit binary number. The 8-bit number is formed by prefixing the 7-bit number by 1 (because there is one -128 in the given negative number).

Note that -1 in denary is $-128 + 127$ and so is equal to 1111 1111 in 2's complement representation.

Activity 29 (Self assessment)

(a) What denary number is equivalent to each of the following 2's complement numbers:

  (i) 1011 0111

  (ii) 0101 1011?

(b) What is the 8-bit 2's complement equivalent of the denary numbers

  (i) 25

  (ii) −96

  (iii) −2?

Comment

The answer is at the end of Block 1.

In the 2's complement system, if an 8-bit word is used, the largest positive number that can be represented is 0111 1111, which is +127, and the largest negative number that can be represented is 1000 0000, which is −128. In total, 127 positive numbers, zero and 128 negative numbers – that is, 256 different numbers – can be represented, which is to be expected from eight bits.

If more than eight bits are used then a greater range of numbers can be represented. For instance, a 16-bit word can represent signed integers in the range −32 768 to +32 767.

In the case of a 16-bit number the leftmost bit, in this case bit 15, again acts as a sign bit. The weighting of this bit is -2^{15} and the weightings of the remaining fifteen bits are 2^{14}, 2^{13}, ..., 2^{0}.

Activity 30 (Exploratory)

You saw in Section 9.1 that 12 bits would be needed to encode the positive values 0 to 3000 if the kitchen scales worked with only positive integer numbers of grams. But of course they work with both positive and negative integers, and so the computer must be able to cope with this. What is the smallest number of bits that is needed to encode the signed integers −3000 to +3000?

Comment

Did you spot that the number of bits is simply one more than the 12 needed for positive integers because twice as many values now need to be represented? So 13 bits would be sufficient. In practice, of course, the computer will simply use two 8-bit words.

9.4 Representing weights

A physical quantity such as weight has the property that it can take on any value, not just a finite set of values. For instance, at one time the ingredients in the scalepan could weigh 29.2569427 grams, at another time 125.1234659 grams, at yet another 2805.87625922 grams. It may not be possible for the scales to display such values, but they are physically possible. Quantities like weight whose values can take on any value in this way are said to be **analogue**.

analogue

Figure 19 may help to make this clearer for you, as it is a diagrammatic representation of an analogue quantity. At the top it shows a number line with gradations from 1 to 10. You can think of this as an analogue quantity that can vary in value between 0 and 10. Numbers between, say, 5 and 6 (such as 5.1 or 5.9) exist on the number line at the top of Figure 19, though they have not been explicitly picked out. You can see they exist if you look at the magnified number line between 5 and 6, where the gradations explicitly show 5.1, 5.2, etc. But numbers between, say, 5.5 and 5.6 also exist on this line, though they have not been explicitly picked out, as you can see on the even-more-magnified number line at the bottom of Figure 19. And this process could go on indefinitely, using greater and greater magnifications to see finer and finer distinctions. There are no breaks or gaps in the line that will be revealed by some increased magnification. And this is exactly what is true of an analogue quantity: there are no breaks or gaps in the values it can take.

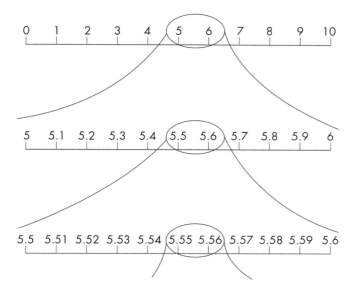

Figure 19 A diagrammatic representation of an analogue quantity

Figure 19 also serves to show the problem that arises when an analogue quantity is to be represented digitally, because the digital representation is rather like the markers along the lines of Figure 19: it can only take one of a set of finite values. If in a particular digital representation only the values 0, 0.1, 0.2, 0.3, ... 1.0, 1.1, 1.2, ... up to 10.0 are possible then an *analogue* value such as 5.53 (see the bottom line in Figure 19), which lies between 5.5 and 5.6, will have to be represented *digitally* by either 5.5 or 5.6. (In practice, 5.5 would be used as it is closer.)

Returning to the example of the kitchen scales, the fact that weight is an analogue quantity presents the difficulty I have just discussed when it is to be represented digitally: its value cannot be represented exactly. So a design decision has to be taken as to how exact the weight's representation is to be (to the nearest 10 grams? to the nearest gram? to the nearest 0.1 grams?), and a number of bits has to be allocated accordingly.

As you have already seen, in metric mode the scales weigh to the nearest gram. Hence they represent 29.2569427 grams as 29 grams, 125.1234659 as 125 grams and 2805.87625922 grams as 2806 grams. The infinitely large number of possible values between 0 and 3000 grams has been cut down to just 3001 values – the integer numbers of grams between 0 and 3000 inclusive.

quantisation
quantisation interval

quantisation error

The process of segmenting an analogue quantity such as weight into a finite number of values is known as **quantisation**, and the gap between consecutive values is known as the **quantisation interval**. (In the case of the scales, the quantisation interval is 1 gram.) The difference between the exact weight to be represented and the nearest of the finite number of values which can represent it is known as the **quantisation error**. In the above example of the scales, the largest possible quantisation error is ±0.5 grams because no actual weight value is more than half a gram from an integer number of grams. Figure 20 illustrates the idea of quantisation. The red lines represent the digital values that the scales work with. They are integer numbers of grams, and you can see that the quantisation interval is 1 gram. Any value from 29.5 grams up to just under 30.5 grams will be quantised to 30 grams, so the maximum quantisation error is ±0.5 grams.

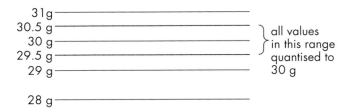

Figure 20　The quantisation interval is 1 gram and the largest possible quantisation error is ±0.5 grams

Reducing the quantisation error

The quantisation error can be made smaller by using a larger number of bits to represent values of the analogue quantity.

You already know that, because the kitchen scales are to weigh up to 3000 g to the nearest gram, 3001 different (positive) weight values are to be represented in the computer and 12 bits are needed to represent each possible value. But suppose the manufacturers had decided to represent weights to the nearest 0.1 gram instead of the nearest gram. Then there would be around ten times as many possible (positive) weight values to represent: 30 001, to be exact. Now, fifteen bits are needed to hold 30 001 different values – that's 3 extra bits per value. So the quantisation error has been reduced by reducing the quantisation interval. This means that the weight is being represented more closely, but at the expense of using more bits to hold the binary code.

Whether this is worthwhile in any particular situation will depend on why the values are being recorded and what they will be used for. In the case of domestic kitchen scales it is unlikely that recipes will call for less than whole numbers of grams, but in a delicate laboratory experiment it may be necessary to measure and record values not just to the nearest 0.1 gram but to the nearest 0.001 gram.

A further complication with representing weights arises from the fact that the weight in the scalepan may be changing. Some of the changes are sudden and isolated, for example when the user places a slab of butter into the scales to weigh it. Other changes may be ongoing, for example when the user slowly adds flour to the scalepan until a required weight has been achieved. Clearly it is necessary to take measurements sufficiently often, and to represent each measurement separately. Measurements taken at intervals are called **samples**. In order to decide how often samples need to be taken (another design decision), it is necessary to know how rapidly the weight is likely to be varying and also what the user will feel comfortable with. For the kitchen scales, probably every tenth of a second or so would be an appropriate rate at which to sample. In some industrial situations it may be necessary to sample much more frequently – or it may be adequate to sample much less frequently.

sample

Although I have focused on representing weights in this section, what I have said is also applicable to a whole range of other physical quantities: for example, temperature, length, pressure, etc. Bear this in mind as you try Activity 31.

Activity 31 (Self assessment)

A particular computer is designed to record the temperature of an oven in an industrial process to the nearest 0.1 °C. The temperature can vary from 200 °C to 250 °C.

(a) What is the quantisation interval?

(b) How many different finite values could a temperature sample take, and how many bits are needed to represent this number of finite values?

(c) What is the largest possible quantisation error?

Comment

The answer is at the end of Block 1.

9.5   Representing true/false quantities

Sometimes a quantity that is to be represented in a computer has only two possible values, either *true* or *false*. An example of such a true/false quantity in the kitchen scales is the one that represents whether the scales are to weigh in metric or in imperial measure. The value of this true/false quantity is given by the true/false response to the statement 'the most recent push of the input button made the measuring system metric'.

Activity 32 (Exploratory)

The beeper on the timer facility on the scales is either on (sounding) or off (silent). The value of a true/false quantity can be used to represent whether it is on or off. What do you think the statement is that will generate true/false responses for the state of the beeper?

Comment

It could be 'the beeper is on'. Then, if the response is true, the true/false quantity will be true and the beeper will be sounding; if it is false the true/false quantity will be false and the beeper will be silent.

Note that an alternative is that the statement is 'the beeper is off'. It is up to the designers to decide which statement is more appropriate in the system and then design the rest of the system to correspond.

True/false quantities such as these are very readily represented by a single bit; all that's needed is to decide whether 1 represents 'true' or 'false'.

Some computers use a single word to hold the value of a true/false quantity, in which case a decision has to be made as to which of the bits in the word is the one that will change depending on whether the value is true or false.

An 8-bit word can, however, hold the values of eight separate true/false quantities if required, making a very compact data representation. This idea could be used for the seven-segment displays in the kitchen scales (look back to Figures 7 and 8 in Section 5 if you need to remind yourself what seven-segment displays look like). Suppose that each individual segment is numbered as shown in Figure 21(a). Note that most seven-segment displays, including the one used in the kitchen scales, have a decimal point, so I have included one in the figure.

The state of each segment can be represented by the true/false quantity implied by the truthfulness of the statement 'the segment is lit'. If 1 represents *true* and 0 represents *false* then the state of the eight segments when displaying the digit 3 (see Figure 21b) would be:

segment 0 = 0

segment 1 = 1

segment 2 = 1

segment 3 = 0

segment 4 = 1

segment 5 = 1

segment 6 = 0

segment 7 = 1

Figure 21 (a) Numbering the segments of a seven-segment display; (b) the seven-segment display showing the digit 3

The segments represented by bits 1, 2, 4, 5 and 7 are on; the others are off. This is encoded in very compactly one word as:

7	6	5	4	3	2	1	0	segment
7	6	5	4	3	2	1	0	bit number
1	0	1	1	0	1	1	0	

Boolean variable

A true/false quantity like the ones I have been describing in this section is sometimes called a **Boolean variable**. Hence a Boolean variable is one whose value will be either *true* or *false*.

Activity 33 (Self assessment)

At one time the seven-segment display is showing the digit 2. How would this be represented using the same convention as in the text above?

Comment

The answer is at the end of Block 1.

9.6   Input and output considerations

So far in Section 9 I have focused on how the data is represented, or encoded, inside the weighing-scales computer. But how does it get into the computer? And how does it get out again in a form that users can recognise? These are big questions, and ones that later parts of the course will be going into in some detail. But I can sketch some answers here.

Weight is the most important input in the kitchen scales. To detect a weight, sensors are placed under the scalepan. They produce an electrical output whose magnitude depends on the magnitude of the weight in the scalepan. This electrical output is fed to the input subsystem. One of the tasks of the input subsystem is to sample the electrical output of the sensors and convert the value it finds to another electrical signal, one that is digital (and therefore quantised). The other task of the input subsystem is to encode this digital signal as a binary number which represents the weight.

A device that converts an analogue input to a digital output is called an **analogue-to-digital converter** or simply an **A–D converter**, and the conversion process is called **analogue-to-digital conversion** or simply **A–D conversion**. The input subsystem must therefore include an analogue-to-digital converter.

analogue-to-digital converter
A–D converter
analogue-to-digital conversion
A–D conversion

Other inputs to the scales come in the form of button presses. Button presses simply close an electrical contact (a switch) and so cause an electrical current to flow. The associated input subsystem encodes this accordingly, perhaps as a 0 for off (no current) and 1 for on (current flowing). The system will have a true/false quantity associated with each button, and will retrieve the value of this quantity from the appropriate input subsystem and store it for use.

The display panel is the most important output of the scales, and you saw in Section 9.5 how a set of true/false quantities representing the on/off states of a seven-segment display could be packed into a single 8-bit word. One such 8-bit word is associated with each seven-segment display on the display panel. All the processor has to do is set each 8-bit word to the correct pattern of 1s and 0s, and send them to the display's output subsystem. The display will then light up correspondingly.

The other output is a sound in the form of a simple beep. Once again a true/false quantity is used and its value is sent to the beeper's output subsystem to make the beeper sound or not sound, as appropriate.

transducer

Transducers

A similar process to the one outlined above occurs when *any* analogue physical quantity is to be represented: a sensor will detect the magnitude of the physical quantity at any pre-determined instant and convert it to an analogue electrical value which is then fed to an analogue-to-digital converter. There are various types of sensors for converting physical quantities to electrical signals: not just for weight, but also for temperature, length, pressure, humidity, and so on. The name **transducer** is commonly given to such sensors.

10 Representing data in the digital camera

Digital cameras need to represent still pictures digitally, and this means that I need to introduce you to how still images are represented. I shall do this in Section 10.1.

The representation of still images generates a very large amount of data. In fact, the data is very seldom stored in its 'raw' form in a computer; instead the data is 'compressed' – that is, made to take up less storage space – before it is stored. I shall discuss the idea of compression in Section 10.2.

Finally, in Section 10.3, I'll look briefly at the ways in which input and output are handled so that the computer can obtain the data it uses and subsequently present the user with appropriate data.

Incidentally, digital cameras also need to represent the state of various true/false quantities, for example whether the user has set the flash on or off. But I shall not discuss true/false quantities further here as you have already done sufficient work on them in Section 9.5.

10.1 Representing still images

There are two basic methods of representing still images in a computer: **bit maps** (also sometimes called raster graphics or raster images) and **vector graphics** (also sometimes called geometrical-shape graphics or graphics metafiles). Bit maps are usually used when there is a great deal of detail, as in photographs, or when there are irregular shapes, such as in drawings of natural objects. Vector graphics are usually reserved for line and blocked-colour drawings consisting of regular shapes. Examples of drawings for which it is appropriate to use vector graphics are flow charts, bar charts, engineering diagrams, etc.

bit map
vector graphic

Activity 34 (Exploratory)

From the foregoing brief descriptions, which method of representing still images do you think that the digital camera will use?

Comment

It will use bit maps, because the images are photographs and so will have a great deal of detail.

Whether an image is obtained by taking a photograph with a digital camera or obtained by scanning a picture, the process of representing it digitally is similar. It involves dividing the image up into a grid of tiny squares called **pixels** (another name is 'pels' – both are abbreviations for 'picture element'). Each pixel is then given a binary code representing its brightness and colour (or its shade of grey if it is a black and white image). This process is known as **digitisation**.

pixel

digitisation

To give you an idea of the process, Figure 22 shows a bit-map representation for a very simple image – one that is purely black and white. Here each pixel can be represented by one bit: 1 for black and 0 for white, as in Figure 22(b). Notice, though, what happens where the grid cuts across the black/white boundary: if 50% or more of the square is black a 1 is used, otherwise a 0 is used. Clearly some of the detail of the original is lost in the digitisation process. When the image is reproduced, as in Figure 22(c), it will have jagged edges. This unwanted effect is sometimes called **pixellation**. Clearly, the smaller the pixels used the less the loss of detail will be apparent to the human eye and the closer the digital representation will seem to the original.

pixellation

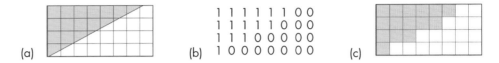

Figure 22   A simple bit-map representation: (a) the original image with a grid of small squares superimposed; (b) the bit-map representation of the original image (1 represents black and 0 represents white); (c) the image which will be reproduced from the bit map

Figure 23(a) shows a black and white photograph reproduced as accurately as possible. Figure 23(b) shows how the photograph would look if it were digitised with a grid of 50 squares per inch. There is obviously some degradation of the image, but it is just about possible to see what the picture is. Figure 23(c) shows how it would look if it were digitised with a grid of just 10 squares per inch. You can clearly see the 'blocky' pixellation effect in this image – in fact the image is so pixellated that it is meaningless.

Figure 23   (a) A black and white photograph of the interior of the casing for a PC, showing some of the sockets and cables; (b) the same photograph digitised at 50 squares per inch; (c) the same photograph digitised at 10 squares per inch

With colour images, if the brightness and colour change over the tiny square, as they very often will, then the binary code for that square will represent an average value for the pixel. This will again result in pixellation and hence some loss of detail when the image is reproduced.

As with black and white images, the smaller the pixels used the closer the digital representation will seem to the original. Similarly, if only a few possible brightnesses and colours are used to represent each pixel then detail will again be lost and the digitised image will only approximate to the original. This time the remedy is to use more brightness values and colours. But increasing the number of pixels (by making each one smaller) means that more code words are needed to represent the image, and increasing the number of brightness values and colours means that each code word needs more bits. The result is that accurate bit-map representations of colour images (or even greyscale ones) need very large numbers of bits indeed and so form very large files. A compromise may have to be made between the file size and the closeness of the representation.

Example 4

A colour picture which is 2 inches by 3 inches[5] is to be bit-mapped at a density of 300 pixels per inch. A total of 256 brightness values and colours will be represented. How many bytes will this produce?

Answer

The 2-inch side will have 600 pixels and the 3-inch side 900. So there are 600×900 pixels in all, which is 540 000. 256 brightness values and colours will need 8 bits to represent them (remember: 256 is 2^8), which is 1 byte. Hence each pixel needs 1 byte and 540 000 bytes in total are needed. That's about half a million bytes – half a megabyte – for just one small picture!

In fact, 256 colour and brightness values aren't really enough to represent a full-colour image satisfactorily, and so in practice 3 bytes are often used to hold the brightness and colour. That increases the number of bytes for a small 2–inch by 3-inch picture to around one and a half million. As you can see, file sizes for images can be very large indeed, and that is why compression is frequently used, as I'll describe shortly.

Activity 35 (Self assessment)

The digital camera introduced in this block produces images that are 2272 by 1712 pixels. Thirty bits are required to represent the colour and brightness data for each pixel. How much memory, in bytes, is required to store a single picture, assuming no compression?

Comment

The answer is at the end of Block 1.

---

[5] Pixel densities are conventionally described 'per inch' and so I have given the picture size in inches as well, to make the arithmetic easier.

Vector graphics

The alternative method of representing images, vector graphics, describes them by their shape. For example, a 2 cm square could be described as follows:

> Starting at the bottom left-hand corner, draw a 2 cm line vertically upwards.
>
> Draw a 2 cm line horizontally towards the right from the top of the previous line.
>
> Draw a 2 cm line vertically downwards from the end of the second line.
>
> Draw a 2 cm line from the end of the third line to the start of the first line.

By using an (x, y) co-ordinate system, this can be condensed to:

> start a new shape at (0,0)
>
> draw line to (0,2)
>
> draw line to (2,2)
>
> draw line to (2,0)
>
> draw line to start point.

Details such as the thickness and colour of the lines, whether the square is to be filled with colour and so on also need to be specified, but even so you can see that this representation is much more compact than the bit-map representation, and so will normally lead to smaller file sizes. But of course this representation does depend on the image being easy to break down into a number of standard shapes (rectangles, straight lines, simple curves, ovals, etc.).

10.2 Compression

The previous section mentioned the large file size of bit-map representations of even small pictures. Therefore just a few images use up a great deal of storage space. This can be inconvenient for PC users, but in the case of a digital camera it presents a real problem. In addition, it is becoming increasingly popular to send digital pictures as e-mail attachments, or via mobile phones using multimedia messaging services (MMS), but large files take a long time to transmit.

The way round the problem of inconveniently large files is to perform manipulations on the data file which represents the image so as to make the file smaller. Put bluntly, some of the 0s and 1s are removed from the file. But of course this is not done arbitrarily; instead it is done very carefully such that the original image can be reproduced when desired.

compression

The process of re-coding data into a more compressed form is called **compression**, and almost any sort of binary data can be compressed. There are various algorithms (sets of rules) for carrying out the compression, each designed to work effectively with a particular type or types of data.

Notice that the advantage of a smaller file is gained at the expense of more processing, because the computer has to perform the algorithm needed to compress the data. Very likely it will also, at some later date, need to perform the algorithm needed to decompress the data.

The size of the original file divided by the size of the compressed file is known as the **compression ratio**. So if, for example, compression techniques could reduce the 540 000 bytes needed for the picture in Example 4 to just 54 000 bytes the compression ratio would be 10. Such compression ratios for pictures are clearly worth having, and they are achievable.

compression ratio

For still pictures such as those in the camera, a very common compression technique known as **JPEG** is used. (JPEG is very common because it is also used for images on the Web.) JPEG is pronounced 'jay-peg' and stands for Joint Photographic Experts Group, the group who devised this standard for compression. This compression technique divides a picture up into small blocks of pixels and performs complex calculations to arrive at a reasonably accurate but concise description of the block. One interesting point about JPEG is that the original data can never be recovered exactly – only an approximation to the original can be recovered. This might sound alarming, but in fact it exploits human physiological characteristics. The human eye simply does not detect some degradation in images, and so is unaware of the effects of the compression process. JPEG can achieve compression ratios of 10 to 20 with no visible loss of quality and ratios of 30 to 50 if some loss of quality is acceptable.

JPEG

A compression technique like JPEG, where the original cannot be recovered exactly afterwards, is known as a **lossy compression** technique.

lossy compression

Lossless compression

Some compression techniques allow the original data to be recovered exactly. These are known as **lossless compression** techniques. These techniques are used, for example, for text files where it is important that no data is lost.

lossless compression

Two common lossless compression techniques are called run-length encoding and the LZ algorithm. These techniques can achieve compression ratios of around 3 or 4 on text.

Simple graphics files can be compressed with a compression technique known as GIF. This is a lossless compression provided the graphics file uses only 8-bit colour; otherwise the GIF algorithm reduces the colours in the image to the 256 possible with 8-bit colour. With GIF, compression ratios of well over 10 can be achieved for simple images. But an attempt to use GIF to compress more complex graphics files may actually increase the file size! In such cases JPEG – and hence lossy compression – is needed.

10.3 Input and output considerations

Earlier in this block, in Section 5.3, you met the idea that the digital camera has a detector which consists of an array of tiny charge-coupled devices (CCDs), which are photosensitive cells. Here I want to expand on this idea a little.

CCDs are not inherently able to detect colour, only brightness. So it is necessary to rely on the fact that any colour of light can be made up from the three primary colours of light: red, blue and green.[6] Each CCD in the array is therefore overlaid with a red, blue or green filter and so detects the brightness of, respectively, the red light, the blue light or the green light falling on it. The filters are arranged in a mosaic pattern, and later processing has to recombine the outputs of groups of CCDs to arrive at the colour of the light in that general area. Figure 24 illustrates this idea for a very small array of CCDs.

R	G	R	G	R	G	R	G
G	B	G	B	G	B	G	B
R	G	R	G	R	G	R	G
G	B	G	B	G	B	G	B
R	G	R	G	R	G	R	G
G	B	G	B	G	B	G	B

Figure 24 The red (R), blue (B) and green (G) filters are laid out in a mosaic pattern over the CCDs; a group of four CCDs is highlighted

You will notice that in Figure 24 there are twice as many green filters as red or blue ones (because the human eye is not equally sensitive to the three primary colours of light). So in fact it is the outputs of groups of *four* CCDs which must be combined to find the colour of light in that general area, as indicated in Figure 24.

Each CCD in the array produces an analogue electrical output that corresponds to the brightness of the filtered light falling on it. Each CCD's output has to be converted to digital form by an A–D converter, and then groups of outputs are processed to arrive at the original colour of the light. Finally, the overall colour and brightness of each pixel is encoded.

You might imagine that the number of pixels in the image will correspond to the number of groups of four CCDs in the array, but actually this is not necessarily the case. First, by averaging values obtained for different groups of four CCDs it is possible to arrive at a one-to-one correspondence between the number of CCDs and the number of pixels, as Figure 25 illustrates. And just to complicate things further, it is possible to create an image with more pixels by 'guessing' intermediate colour and brightness values between adjacent CCDs.

From the foregoing you will be able to see that there is a great deal of processing associated with the production of a bit-map image from the CCD array's output – and I have not even mentioned the compression that will take place. For this reason many digital cameras, including the

---

[6] Note that the three primary colours of light are different from the three primary colours of pigments.

R	G	R	G	R	G	R	G
G	B	G	B	G	B	G	B
R	G	R	G	R	G	R	G
G	B	G	B	G	B	G	B
R	G	R	G	R	G	R	G
G	B	G	B	G	B	G	B

Figure 25 The colour and brightness value of the blue (B) 'cell' four along and four down can be deduced by averaging the values obtained from the four highlighted groups of four 'cells', each of which has this blue 'cell' in one corner

one described in this block, contain a second processor. This second processor is a **digital signal processor** or **DSP**, which is a processor specially designed for repetitive yet demanding tasks like image processing.

**digital signal processor
DSP**

So far as output is concerned, the camera provides a screen on which the user can view photos already taken, and also the shot about to be taken. The output process of showing images on this screen works as follows. The screen, which is backlit, consists of an array of tiny liquid crystals that can be made transparent or opaque in response to electrical signals. It is therefore known as a **liquid-crystal display** or **LCD**. To make the display coloured, the liquid crystals are grouped in threes, one with a red filter, one with a blue and one with a green. The LCD's associated output subsystem receives colour and brightness data from the processor and sends appropriate electrical signals to control the transparency of the liquid crystals on the screen.

**liquid-crystal display
LCD**

CMOS image sensors

The digital camera discussed in this block uses an array of CCDs to capture the colour and brightness of the image. An alternative method of capturing the colour and brightness is to use what is known as a CMOS image sensor. These sensors are made using the same technology as silicon chips and can therefore be integrated onto the same chip as a processor, which can be very convenient in small portable items such as cameras.

CMOS image sensors consist of arrays of light-sensitive cells, and in some cases groups of cells are used to detect red, blue and green light (much as for CCDs). One manufacturer, however, has patented a process which has a big advantage over CCDs: each individual cell can be made to detect the brightnesses of all three of red, blue and green light. This means that no averaging processes for groups of cells are needed for this manufacturer's CMOS arrays. Against this advantage must be set the disadvantage that more complex circuitry is required to detect the outputs of the cells.

As well as being used in digital cameras, CMOS image sensors are used in some mobile phones and web cams.

11 Representing data in the PC

Personal computers, or PCs, are very versatile computers and can perform a huge range of tasks. So whereas the uses of the kitchen scales and the digital camera indicate clearly what types of data are to be represented, the PC leaves the field very broad indeed. I have therefore chosen to consider some of the data representations used when families and friends use e-mails to keep in touch. Very conveniently, these lead to some different data representations.

At their simplest, e-mails are text only. So I shall look first, in Section 11.1, at how text can be represented.

But people are increasingly exchanging photos, video clips and even sound files via e-mail, using the attachment facility. You already know how still pictures such as photos can be represented, but in this section I shall show you how moving pictures and sound can be represented, in Sections 11.2 and 11.3 respectively.

Finally, in Section 11.4 I will look at relevant input and output considerations for the PC.

11.1 Representing text

Study note: You will need to refer to the T224 Reference Manual while you are working through this section.

Text can be represented in a computer by a succession of binary codes, with each code representing a letter from the alphabet or a punctuation mark. Numerals can also be represented this way, if desired. This can be useful in, say, a word-processing application where no calculations are to be performed and it is convenient to encode a digit in a phrase such as 'we agreed to meet at 7 o'clock' in the same way that all the other characters in the sentence are encoded.

ASCII code

Of course, the binary codes that will be used need to be agreed upon in advance. PCs, in common with many other computers, use a code based on the **ASCII code**[7] (pronounced 'askey') to represent letters and numerals, that is alphanumeric characters, together with certain other symbols found on computer keyboards. The ASCII code, which dates back to the early days of computing, allocates seven bits for each symbol. Because nowadays computers work with 8-bit groups of 1s and 0s (that is, bytes), rather than with 7-bit groups, ASCII codes are often extended by one bit to 8 bits. There is no one standard way of doing this, but the one used in PCs is simply to prefix a 0 to each 7-bit code.

---

[7] ASCII stands for American Standard Code for Information Interchange.

The set of 7-bit ASCII codes is shown in the appendix of the T224 Reference Manual, which you should look at now.

Notice that some of the ASCII codes do not represent a displayable character but instead represent an action (e.g. line feed, tab). These codes are said to represent 'control characters'. Those characters in the range 0000 0000 to 0001 1111 which are not shown in the appendix are all control characters.

Activity 36 (Self assessment)

Write a sequence of binary codes which forms an answer to the following question, using the appendix of your Reference Manual.

0100 1001

0111 0011

0010 0000

0011 0010

0011 1101

0011 0011

0011 1111

Comment

The answer is at the end of Block 1.

A significant problem with ASCII is that it cannot cope with languages that use non-Latin characters, for example the ß character used in German, or several of the Cyrillic characters used in Russian. One solution has been to create national variants of ASCII, but of course this causes problems when files are transferred between different language areas.

A longer-term solution is Unicode, which assigns a unique, standard code for every character in use in the world's major written languages. It also has codes for punctuation marks, diacriticals (such as the tilde ˜ used over some characters in, for example, Spanish), mathematical symbols, and so on. Unicode uses 16 bits, permitting over 65 000 characters to be coded. It also allows for an extension mechanism to enable an additional 1 million characters to be coded.

As far as the Latin alphabet is concerned, there are similarities between ASCII and Unicode. For example, the upper-case letter A in Unicode is represented by

0000 0000 0100 0001

The last 7 bits of this are identical to the 7-bit ASCII code for the same letter.

The software run on PCs is slowly changing over to Unicode instead of 8-bit ASCII.

Sizes of text files

You may want to send a text file as an attachment to your e-mail. But how large will the file be?

Suppose you type about a hundred words of plain text (just one font, no bold, no underlining, no paragraph formatting, etc.) into your word processor and save the resulting document as a file. In English, words average some five or six letters, and there is a space between each word. So you will be saving about seven hundred characters in all, including spaces and punctuation marks. In ASCII, which uses one byte per character, you might expect a resulting file size of around 700 bytes, but as your computer probably rounds up to the nearest kilobyte (a kilobyte is 1024 bytes) you might expect it to record a file size of 1 kilobyte. Even in a language whose average number of letters per word is more than English, you would hardly expect a file size over a kilobyte.

Yet I just tried this with my word processor, and the resulting file size was 20 kilobytes!

Let me hasten to add that when I saved my hundred words as plain text (one of the options offered by my word processor) the text file was indeed 1 kilobyte. So there is nothing wrong with my arithmetic. The difference in the expected and actual file sizes when my word processor saves in its own native format lies in the way the word processor saves files. For instance it adds a great deal of information of its own (who created the file, what it is called, when it was created, how big it is, what font and type size is being used, etc.). It also puts the user's text and its own additional information into chunks whose (pre-defined) size is quite large. These and other similar aspects of what the word processor saves add a considerable overhead into the file size.

So if formatting doesn't matter you might want to consider sending your text file unformatted. If formatting does matter, you have the option of using a lossless compression technique (such as 'Zip') to reduce your file size by a factor of perhaps 3 or 4.

11.2 Representing moving images

A moving image is simply a series of still images presented at sufficiently short time intervals that the eye smoothes over the change from one image to the next. In practice, this means the images must change at a minimum rate of around 20 per second; if the rate is lower then the moving image flickers or is jerky. Each still image that goes to make up a moving image is known as a **frame**.

frame

So far as computers are concerned, moving images are of two types. One type is **animations** and the other is **videos** (also known as **films** or **movies** or **video clips**). The essential difference between a video and an animation is that in a video the images will have been captured by some sort of camera whereas in an animation they will have been drawn, probably with the assistance of a computer. These days the difference is

animation
video
film
movie
video clip

becoming blurred because videos can be heavily altered by computer techniques and animations can be made to look very lifelike indeed, so animations and video can be merged into a single frame.

In Section 10.1 you saw that even as small a full-colour image as 3 inches by 2 inches can need 1.5 megabytes to represent it if it is uncompressed. At the minimum of 20 frames per second, a 5-minute video clip (300 seconds) will need 1.5 × 300 × 20 megabytes = 9000 megabytes of storage space! So compression is even more necessary here than it is for still images.

For moving pictures, a lossy compression technique called **MPEG** ('em-peg', which stands for Motion Picture Experts Group) is often used. MPEG uses methods similar to those of JPEG for each frame in the sequence, but performs further compression from one frame to the next by taking advantage of the fact that often the next frame is only slightly changed from the previous (e.g. someone has moved slightly against an unchanging background). A compressed MPEG file would therefore not include data to represent the background in the next frame (and possibly not in a few more frames as well), but would simply indicate that certain portions of the picture have not changed from one frame to the next. Further, MPEG may not include some frames at all on compression, and the decompression process would work out what these frames must have been and include them. (This is not as odd as it sounds. Often it is very easy to work out what must have happened between frames. For instance, if an object has moved a short distance then the decompression process will simply assume that the object has moved smoothly and will put it at intermediate positions in the intermediate frames.) MPEG can achieve compression ratios of as much as 50, a compression ratio that is necessary if a full-length film is to be fitted onto a DVD.

MPEG

Activity 37 (Self assessment)

The digital camera you have met frequently in this block can take short sequences of shots (frames) which form a very brief 'video clip'. If the clip comprises 100 frames, the screen is 2272 pixels by 1712 pixels and 30 bits are used to represent the colour and brightness of each pixel, how many bytes would this video clip occupy if it was uncompressed? How many would it occupy if each individual frame in the clip was compressed with JPEG at a compression ratio of 20? How many would it occupy if instead MPEG was used on the whole clip, at a compression ratio of 50?

Comment

The answer is at the end of Block 1.

If you were thinking of e-mailing the video clip described in Activity 37 to a friend, you and your friend would both be very grateful indeed for compression techniques!

11.3   Representing sound

Sound, such as speech or music, is an analogue physical quantity that varies with time, and so the ideas you have already met in Section 9.4

about converting analogue weights to digital form are relevant here too. In particular, samples of the sound will have to be taken, and each sample will have to be quantised to the nearest binary code in the digital representation.

It's important to appreciate that sound such as speech or music varies rapidly with time, and so samples of it will have to be taken at very closely spaced intervals if the digital representation is to be faithful to the original.

frequency

Before I can talk about how closely the samples must be spaced, I need to introduce the idea of the **frequency** of sound. A sound of high frequency is one that people hear as a high-pitched sound; a sound of low frequency is one that people hear as one of low-pitched sound. Sound consists of air vibrations, and it is the rate at which the air vibrates that determines the frequency: a higher vibration rate is a higher frequency. So if the air vibrates at, say, 100 cycles per second then the frequency of the sound is said to be 100 cycles per second. The unit of 1 cycle per second is given the name 'hertz', abbreviated to 'Hz'. Hence a frequency of 100 cycles per second is normally referred to as a frequency of 100 Hz.

sampling theorem

So how often must the sound be sampled? There is a rule called the **sampling theorem** which says that if the frequencies in the sound range from 0 to B Hz then, for a faithful representation, the sound must be sampled at a rate greater than $2B$ samples per second.

Example 5

The human ear can detect frequencies in music up to around 20 kHz (that is, 20 000 Hz). What sampling rate is needed for a faithful digital representation of music? What is the time interval between successive samples?

Answer

20 kHz is 20 000 Hz, and so the B in the text above the question is 20 000. The sampling theorem therefore says that the music must be sampled more than 2 × 20 000 samples per second, which is more than 40 000 samples per second.

If 40 000 samples are being taken each second, they must be 1/40 000 seconds apart. This is 0.000025 seconds, which is 0.025 milliseconds (thousandths of a second) or 25 microseconds (millionths of a second).

The answer to Example 5 shows the demands made on a computer if music is to be faithfully represented. Samples of the music must be taken at intervals of less than 25 microseconds. And each of those samples must be stored by the computer.

If speech is to be represented then the demands can be less stringent, first because the frequency range of the human voice is smaller than that of music (up to only about 12 kHz) and second because speech is recognisable even when its frequency range is quite severely restricted. (For example, some digital telephone systems sample at only 8000 samples per second, thereby cutting out most of the higher-frequency components of the human voice, yet we can make sense of what the speaker on the other end of the phone says, and even recognise their voice.)

Activity 38 (Self assessment)

(a) Five minutes of music is sampled at 40 000 samples per second, and each sample is encoded into 16 bits (2 bytes). How big will the resulting music file be?

(b) Five minutes of speech is sampled at 8000 samples per second, and each sample is encoded into 16 bits (2 bytes). How big will the resulting speech file be?

Comment

The answer is at the end of Block 1.

You answer to Activity 38 has probably convinced you that speech and, especially, music files are not the sort of thing you wish to send as an e-mail attachment! Fortunately there is a compression technique that can be used for sound files. It is known as **MP3**, which is short for 'MPEG-1 Audio layer 3', indicating that it is a compression technique defined in the first version of the MPEG standard. Using MP3, compression ratios up to about 12 can be achieved without any noticeable degradation of the sound quality. Higher compression ratios can be achieved if some loss of quality can be tolerated – as much as 100 if telephone-quality speech is acceptable.

MP3

11.4 Input and output considerations

In this final portion of Section 11, I shall look in outline at how text, moving pictures and sound can be input into a PC and output from it. I'll leave aside the possibility that the data has been obtained by buying a disk or downloading via the Internet and assume that the user is creating it.

I'll start by considering text, typed in at the keyboard. Pressing a key closes a contact and causes electrical current to flow. This enables the computer's keyboard input system to detect which key has been pressed. The input subsystem then generates a corresponding internal code – which is neither

---

Music CDs

Music CDs do rather better than the 40 000 samples per second suggested by Example 5; they are created by taking 44 100 samples every second for each of the two stereo channels, which means that the interval between samples is just under 23 microseconds per channel.

They use 16 bits to hold each sample, which is enough to make the quantisation error imperceptible to human ears when the digital sound is replayed.

The files that result from this sampling rate and number of bits are large. One of the standard sizes of music CD – the one that runs for 80 minutes – holds over 800 million bytes.

the PC's version of ASCII nor Unicode but which is predefined for PC keyboards – and sends this code to the processor. From now on it is up to the application to translate this special keyboard code into its own binary codes.

Next I'll consider the input of moving images. For this it's convenient to use a simple digital camcorder, perhaps a web cam. Such a camera produces a stream of frames, each one produced either from a CCD array, in the same way as you saw for the digital camera, or (as is becoming increasingly likely) from a CMOS detector. There is a great deal of processing to be done here (for each brightness and colour value for each pixel of each frame, and probably compression as well so that the resulting data does not take up too much space) and so the input subsystem needs to incorporate a processor. Some web cams now incorporate their own input subsystem; for others a special video capture card in the PC is used as the input subsystem.

So far as sound is concerned, the user may speak into a microphone. In this case the microphone converts the vibrations in the air which are the speech signal into an electrical signal which is fed into an input subsystem on the computer's sound card. The sound card performs the necessary sampling and analogue-to-digital conversion and produces a stream of binary codes representing the sound for the PC's processor. Alternatively, the user may feed a pre-recorded analogue sound signal directly to the sound card, which again performs the necessary sampling and analogue-to-digital conversion.

All of the above are inputs to the PC. What about the reproduction of text, moving images and sounds by the PC?

Most PCs have three ways of reproducing these sorts of data: the screen (text and moving images); a printer (text); one or more loudspeakers (sound).

To produce a display on a PC's screen it is necessary to convert the binary codes for the image into corresponding colour and brightness levels for every pixel on the screen. These colour and brightness levels are then used to produce the required display – whether of text or images. If moving images are to be displayed then the image on the screen needs to be updated often enough for the user to perceive the motion as fluid, rather than jerky. As you have already seen, this implies a minimum rate of about 20 images per second.

The task of getting exactly the right colour and brightness for each pixel on the screen is an enormously demanding one for the output subsystem, and so PCs have a video card in them which contains a processor dedicated to just this one task.

Text characters are printed on paper as patterns of tiny dots of ink. Hence to produce a page of printed text it is necessary to convert each text character to an appropriate dot pattern and thus create the dot pattern for the whole page. A laser printer puts a whole line of tiny dots onto the page simultaneously, but an ink-jet printer sweeps repeatedly across the page, producing each line dot by dot. Most output subsystems associated with printers now incorporate a processor to help with the printing tasks.

To produce sounds, the opposite process to analogue-to-digital conversion is needed, starting from the codes that represent the sounds. As you might expect, this process is called **digital-to-analogue conversion** or **D–A conversion**. A digital-to-analogue converter forms part of the output subsystem for the PC's loudspeaker(s). This output subsystem is usually located on the computer's sound card, and its analogue output signal is fed to the loudspeaker(s) to produce the sound.

digital-to-analogue conversion
D–A conversion

Creating drawings and paintings

To create a drawing electronically, a drawing package can be used. This will detect the user's mouse movements, together with their menu choices for colour, weight of line, etc., and use these inputs to generate a vector graphics file.

Alternatively, a paint package can be used. Here the user's mouse movements and menu choices will be detected and used to generate a bit map.

A third alternative is to draw or paint the picture on paper by hand and then scan it. In this case the scanner will divide the picture up into pixels and then work systematically across and down the picture, using CCDs with filters to capture the colour and brightness of each pixel and then digitising and encoding these values. This process will form a bit map of the picture. Most scanners then compress the image, offering the user a choice of which compression technique to use.

12 Representing data in computers: conclusion

Study note: You will need to refer to the T224 Reference Manual while you are working through this section.

There is one very important type of data that I need to introduce before I leave this topic of representing data in computers. This type of data didn't fit neatly into just one of Sections 9, 10 or 11 because it is a type found in *all* computers. This data type relates to the computer programs that enable the processor to carry out tasks. A computer program that is ready to be executed on a processor will be in the form of a long list of **computer instructions**, and you will not be surprised to learn that each computer instruction is encoded as one or more binary words.

computer instruction

Every make and model of processor is designed to have a particular set of instructions which it can execute, and one of the tasks of the processor's designers is to decide which binary code will represent each of these instructions.

Most programmers, however, do not need to be aware of the binary codes that represent the processor's instructions when they write a program. This is because there are computer programs called 'compilers' which take a program written in a form easy for humans to work in and translate it into the binary codes the processor needs.

You will meet some computer instructions, and their corresponding binary codes, in Block 2 when you look at how processors work.

The last few sections have demonstrated that every conceivable type of data is encoded in computers in binary form. Did it perhaps occur to you that this means that codes – patterns of 1s and 0s – can stand for different entities in different situations? Take for example the code

    0100 0001

If this code word represents text then it stands for the letter 'A' in the 8-bit ASCII coding scheme. If it represents an integer then it stands for 65 in the natural binary coding scheme. If it represents a set of true/false quantities then it could represent, say, which segments of a seven-segment display were on or off. If it is part of the representation of an image then it will encode a particular level of brightness and/or colour. If it is part of the representation of a computer program then it could represent, say, an instruction to perform an addition.

How does the computer 'know' how to treat a particular code?

The answer to this is that it does exactly what the program tells it to do with each code it meets. The very first code a processor encounters when it is first switched on must be the code for a computer instruction. This will tell the processor what to do next, and so on. From then on the computer will do whatever manipulations it is told to do on every binary code word it is given. It is up to the people who write the program or programs that run on the computer to ensure that the computer is given the right code words, in the right order, and is correctly told what to do with each and every one of them.

This is why software is such a crucial part of a computer system.

Activity 39 (Self assessment)

What would the code word

　　0010 0100

stand for if it is:

(a) the code for an integer using natural binary;

(b) the code for a fixed-point fraction where the binary point is taken to lie between the two groups of 4 bits;

(c) the code for a set of 8 Boolean variables which represent whether the segments of a 7-segment display are on or off (assume the same convention as given in Section 9.5);

(d) the code for a text character using the same 8-bit ASCII code as in a PC?

Comment

The answer is at the end of Block 1.

Activity 40 (Review/Exam preparation)

Now is a good point for you to turn to your *Block 1 Companion* and fill in some more of the spaces in the tables of learning outcomes. Your work in Sections 8 to 12 is relevant to several of the outcomes.

13 Manipulating data in computers: introduction

Sections 8 to 12 of this block have shown that in a computer all types of data are represented by binary codes, and that programmers must make sure that the programs they write treat this data appropriately in any particular application: as text if it is intended to be text, as a binary fraction if it is intended to be a binary fraction, and so on.

Programmers must also ensure that the programs manipulate the binary codes in an appropriate way for the particular application. But what sorts of manipulation are possible inside a computer?

Perhaps surprisingly, a great deal of data manipulation in a computer is simply moving data around without changing it at all. You will see examples of this, and of why it is necessary, in Block 2.

Not so surprisingly, a fair amount of the data manipulation takes the form of arithmetic: addition, subtraction, multiplication and division. For example, some of the lossy compression techniques I mentioned in Sections 10.2 and 11.2 require a great deal of arithmetic. I'll talk more about arithmetic involving binary numbers in Section 14.

testing

Another common manipulation is comparing data (with a view to taking an action that depends on the result of the comparison). This is usually referred to as **testing**. Think for example about a spell-check program that is checking whether a word in the e-mail you have just typed is in its dictionary. The letters in your word and the letters in the word in the dictionary will all be in ASCII format. Pairs of ASCII codes can then be compared systematically, and if the codes in each pair are identical then your word is identical to the word in the dictionary and the spell checker can move on to the next word in your e-mail. If all the codes are not identical then either the computer has yet to find the word you are using, or possibly you have a made spelling mistake, or the word is not in its dictionary. Either way, what the computer does next depends on the outcome of the comparison test. You will meet various sorts of test in Block 2.

The fourth sort of data manipulation, not so common but still used, is logic operations on the data. I'll explain what I mean by logic operations in Section 15, and give an example of how such manipulations could be used.

So there are four basic types of data manipulation carried out in computers:

- moving data around unchanged;
- carrying out arithmetic operations on data;
- testing data;
- carrying out logic operations on data.

Block 2 will revisit these types of operation and discuss them in more detail; here in this block I will focus on arithmetic operations (Section 14) and logic operations (Section 15).

In computers, arithmetic and logic operations are carried out by a crucial component in the processor called an arithmetic–logic unit (ALU). So when you look at arithmetic and logic operations in Sections 14 and 15 you will be looking at the operations carried out by the processor's ALU.

For simplicity, I shall use 8-bit words throughout Sections 14 and 15, but the principles are equally applicable to binary data words of other lengths, and ALUs may indeed be designed to act on 16-, 32- or even 64-bit words.

14 Binary arithmetic

Study note: You may like to have the T224 Numeracy Resource to hand as you study Section 14. It offers extra practice with the manipulations, and you may find this useful.

14.1 Adding unsigned integers

Pairs of binary digits are added according to the rules

$0 + 0 = 0$

$0 + 1 = 1$

$1 + 1 = 10$, which is 0 and carry 1.

This last rule arises from the fact that 10 in binary is the equivalent of denary 2.

In order to be able to add pairs of binary integers which may consist of several bits, one further rule is needed to allow for the fact that a carry may have to be added into a pair of bits. This rule is

$1 + 1 + 1 = 11$

which is 1 and carry 1. (Remember that 11 in binary is equivalent to 3 in denary.)

The following example shows how two 8-bit binary integers are added.

Example 6

Add the 8-bit binary integers 0101 1100 and 0110 1011.

Answer

First the two integers are written in columns under each other:

```
    0   1   0   1   1   1   0   0
+   0   1   1   0   1   0   1   1
  _____
```

Starting with the *rightmost* (least-significant) bit from both integers and using the above rules gives $0 + 1 = 1$, so the rightmost bit of the result is 1. Similarly the next two bits (working from right to left) are also 1. The fourth bit is found from $1 + 1$ and so is 0 with a carry of 1. So far, therefore, the result is:

```
    0   1   0   1   1   1   0   0
+   0   1   1   0   1   0   1   1
  _____
                    0   1   1   1
            1                        (carry)
```

The next bit is found from $1 + 0 + 1$ and so is 0 with a carry of 1. Similarly, the next bit of the result is 0 with another carry of 1. The result so far is:

```
    0   1   0   1   1   1   0   0
+   0   1   1   0   1   0   1   1
   ─────────────────────────────
        0   0   0   1   1   1
    1   1   1                       (carry)
```

The next bit of the result is found from $1+1+1$, which is 1 with a carry of 1. The last (most-significant) bit is therefore $0+0+1$, which is 1. So the final result is:

```
    0   1   0   1   1   1   0   0
+   0   1   1   0   1   0   1   1
   ─────────────────────────────
    1   1   0   0   0   1   1   1
    1   1   1   1                   (carry)
```

Therefore the sum of 0101 1100 and 0110 1011 is 1100 0111.

This can be checked by converting each integer to denary: 0101 1100 is 92, 0110 1011 is 107 and 1100 0111 is 199, which checks.

There is no need to consider the addition of more than two binary integers at once, because in computers integers are generally added two at a time. If three integers are to be added, the first two are added and then the third is added to their sum.

Activity 41 (Self assessment)

(a) Add the 4-bit binary integers 1011 and 0011. Check your result by converting all integers to denary.

(b) Add the 8-bit binary integers 0110 1100 and 0001 0110.

Comment

The answer is at the end of Block 1.

Sometimes when two 8-bit integers are added the result cannot be contained in an 8-bit binary word. An example is:

```
        1   1   0   1   1   0   1   1
+       1   0   1   1   0   0   0   0
   ─────────────────────────────────
    1   1   0   0   0   1   0   1   1
```

where 9 bits are needed to hold the result (because it is greater than denary 255). A similar outcome can occur with binary integers of lengths other than 8 bits. The extra bit generated in the result is called a **carry bit**.[8]

carry bit

The hardware of most processors has a means of indicating that a carry bit has been generated; it is up to the software to ensure that this carry bit is dealt with appropriately.

---

[8] There can, of course, be intermediate carry bits between two adjacent columns of the sum, but when talking about the addition of two binary integers the term 'carry bit' is usually taken to refer to an extra bit generated when the two most-significant bits are added.

14.2   Adding 2's complement integers

The leftmost bit at the start of a 2's complement integer (which represents the presence or absence of the weighting −128) is treated in just the same way as all the other bits in the integers. So the rules given at the start of Section 14.1 for adding unsigned integers can be used.

Example 7

Add the 2's complement integers 1011 1011 and 0010 1011.

Answer

```
    1   0   1   1   1   0   1   1
+   0   0   1   0   1   0   1   1
  ─────────────────────────────────
    1   1   1   0   0   1   1   0
```

(Check: 1011 1011 is −69, 0010 1011 is 43 and 1110 0110 is −26; −69 + 43 does equal −26.)

When two negative integers are added, there will be a ninth bit in the result. The extra bit can be ignored; it is a consequence of using bit 7 as a sign bit.

There is, however, a phenomenon that may occur that cannot be ignored. When two negative integers are added the result must be negative and when two positive integers are added the result must be positive. Sometimes the sign bit appears to change as the result of adding two such integers in 2's complement arithmetic. This occurs when the magnitude of the sum is too big for the seven available bits in the data word and so 'overflows' into the leftmost bit. The consequence of this is that the addition of two positive integers appears to have produced a negative result, or the addition of two negative integers to have produced a positive result. This phenomenon is called **2's complement overflow**.

2's complement overflow

Consider for example the addition of 0111 1000 (denary 120) and 0000 1111 (denary 15). Performing the addition 0111 1000 + 0000 1111 gives 1000 0111, which looks as if it is a negative number (the leftmost bit is 1). Here is a case where 2's complement overflow has occurred. You can see why this has happened if you note that the result should be 135. This is greater than 127, the maximum positive value that can be represented in an 8-bit word in 2's complement form (see Section 9.3).

Some processors detect that 2's complement overflow has occurred, in which case it is up to the software to deal with it. In other processors the programmer has to build in explicit tests to check that 2's complement overflow has not occurred during additions.

14.3   Subtracting 2's complement integers

You will probably have carried out subtraction of denary numbers using rules for subtraction that include the process of 'borrowing' whenever you need to subtract a larger digit from a smaller one. It is possible to perform binary subtraction in a very similar way, but that is not what happens in computers. The processor contains the circuits needed to perform addition, and it is much more efficient to use these circuits also to perform subtraction than it is to build in extra circuits to perform subtraction.

But how can subtraction be converted into addition? The answer is by first converting the number to be subtracted into its additive inverse. For example, the denary subtraction

    7 – 5

can be converted into addition provided the additive inverse of 5 is used. As I mentioned in Section 9.3, the additive inverse of 5 is ⁻5, and so the equivalent addition is

    7 + (⁻5)

In 2's complement binary arithmetic, the additive inverse of a number is known as its **2's complement**. I'll start, therefore, by showing you how to find the 2's complement of any binary number.

2's complement

14.3.1 Finding the 2's complement

In Section 9.3 you saw how to find the 2's complement representation of any given positive or negative denary integer, but it is also useful to be able to find the additive inverse of a 2's complement integer without going into and out of denary. For instance, 1111 1100 (⁻4) is the additive inverse, or 2's complement, of 0000 0100 (+4), but how does one find the additive inverse without converting both binary integers to their denary equivalents?

The answer is that the additive inverse, or 2's complement, of any signed binary integer can be found by a two-step process: first find the complement (1's complement) of the given number and then add 1. **1's complement** or **complement** means that all the 1s are changed to 0s and all the 0s to 1s.

1's complement complement

An example should make this clear.

Example 8

Find the 2's complement of the signed integer 0001 1011.

Answer

First find the complement of the given integer (change all the 1s to 0s and all the 0s to 1s), getting:

    1110 0100

and then add 1 to get:

    1110 0101

So the 2's complement of 0001 1011 is 1110 0101. (Check: the given integer is + 27, and 1110 0101 is ⁻27.)

Activity 42 (Self assessment)

(a) Write down the complement of 1010 0101.

(b) Find the 2's complement of the signed integer 1011 0111. Check your answer by converting both integers to denary.

(c) Find the additive inverse of the signed integer 0000 1111.

Comment

The answer is at the end of Block 1.

14.3.2 Subtraction

As I indicated at the start of this section, subtraction is converted to addition by replacing the number to be subtracted by its additive inverse, which in the case of binary arithmetic is its 2's complement. An example should make this clear.

Example 9

Subtract the signed integer 1010 1010 from the signed integer 0001 0110.

Answer

The additive inverse of the number to be subtracted, 1010 1010, is 0101 0101 + 1 = 0101 0110. Using this additive inverse transforms the computation to an addition:

	0	0	0	1	0	1	1	0
+	0	1	0	1	0	1	1	0
	0	1	1	0	1	1	0	0

(Check: 1010 1010 is −86 and 0001 0110 is 22, so the calculation is 22 − (−86), which is 108, and 0110 1100 is indeed 108.)

Activity 43 (Self assessment)

Carry out the following subtraction by first finding the additive inverse of the number to be subtracted:

　　1100 1010 − 0000 1110

Comment

The answer is at the end of Block 1.

14.4 Multiplying 2's complement integers

Multiplication can be thought of as repeated addition. For instance, in denary arithmetic

　　7 × 5

can be thought of as

　　7 + 7 + 7 + 7 + 7

There is therefore no need for a new process for the multiplication of binary integers; multiplication can be transformed into repeated addition.

In multiplication the result is very often much larger than either of the two integers being multiplied, and so a multiple-length representation may be needed to hold the result of a multiplication. This is something that must be taken care of in any program that will be using multiplication.

In fact, there are some simple ways of reducing the number of steps in the multiplication process. I'll illustrate with a denary example.

To multiply 7 by 15, you could add $7+7$ to get 14, then $14+7$ to get 21, then $21+7$ to get 28, and so on. You would carry out a total of 14 addition operations. Alternatively you could spot that 15 is $10+5$ and that 7×10 is 70 which is simply 7 shifted one place to the left. So you could replace 9 of the additions with one shift to the left, and then do the final 5 additions. This would reduce a total of 14 operations to a total of 6 (one shift and five additions). The reduction in steps would be even more dramatic if the original sum was 7×105, because then a multiplication by 100 can be implemented by two shifts to the left ($7 \times 100 = 700$) followed by 5 additions. This time 104 addition operations have been reduced to two shifts and five additions. Quite a saving!

Similarly, in binary arithmetic, a multiplication by *two* can be implemented by a shift one place to the left, a multiplication by *four* by two shifts to the left, and so on. Just as in denary arithmetic, the vacant space on the right is filled with a 0. So again a judicious mixture of shifts and additions can reduce the number of operations to be performed during a multiplication operation.

Activity 44 (Exploratory)

(a) Perform the binary multiplication 0010 1000 $\times$ 11 by adding 0010 1000 to itself the appropriate number of times.

(b) Perform the binary multiplication 0010 1000 $\times$ 11 by first shifting 0010 1000 one place to the left and then adding 0010 1000.

(c) Which would you say was simpler?

Comment

(a) The first addition will give two (10_2) times 0010 1000:

	0	0	1	0	1	0	0	0
+	0	0	1	0	1	0	0	0
	0	1	0	1	0	0	0	0

and the next addition will give three (11_2) times 0010 1000:

	0	1	0	1	0	0	0	0
+	0	0	1	0	1	0	0	0
	0	1	1	1	1	0	0	0

So the result is 0111 1000.

(b) Shifting 0010 1000 one place to the left (and filling up on the right with a 0) gives 0101 0000. Adding 0010 1000 to this gives (as before):

	0	1	0	1	0	0	0	0
+	0	0	1	0	1	0	0	0
	0	1	1	1	1	0	0	0

(c) I think the second operation was simpler. Do you agree?

14.5 Dividing 2's complement integers

Just as multiplication can be turned into repeated additions, so division can be turned into repeated subtractions. And just as shifting a binary integer one place to the *left* equates to multiplying by two, so shifting a binary integer one place to the *right* equates to dividing by two.

Activity 45 (Exploratory)

How many places to the right do you think you would need to shift a binary integer to achieve division by eight?

Comment

You probably guessed that if shifting one place to the right is dividing by two then shifting two places to the right is dividing by four and shifting three places to the right is dividing by eight. And this is indeed the case.

Note that in integer arithmetic a fractional result is not possible. So if the divisor does not go exactly into the number to be divided then the result will have to be in the form of 'it divides in such-and-such a number of times, with a remainder of such-and-such'.

14.6 Arithmetic with binary fractions

My final point in the preceding section brings home the fact that integer arithmetic is not really suitable when divisions are to be performed. It is also not suitable where some or all of the values involved in the arithmetic are not – or are not necessarily – integers, and this is often the case. In such cases, arithmetic has to be performed on non-integers.

The most common representation for non-integers is the floating-point representation that I mentioned briefly in a box in Section 9.2. You may recall that numbers are represented in the form (mantissa $\times$ 2^{exponent}), where the mantissa is a fixed-point fraction and the exponent a signed integer. Arithmetic with floating-point numbers may therefore involve calculations such as

$$(0.111\ 0001 \times 2^{10}) + (0.000\ 1000 \times 2^{5})$$
$$(1.101\ 1000 \times 2^{-5}) - (1.000\ 1000 \times 2^{-6})$$
$$(0.101\ 1100 \times 2^{15}) \div (0.111\ 0101 \times 2^{-12})$$

Such arithmetic is by no means straightforward, and I have no intention of trying to show you how it is carried out. Most processors destined for PCs, workstations and other powerful computers include a 'floating-point unit' whose sole task is to carry out operations on floating-point numbers. If a processor without a floating-point unit is to be used to perform floating-point arithmetic then the software will have to take care of the complicated manipulations involved.

15 Logic operations

> *Study note: You may like to have the T224 Numeracy Resource to hand as you study Section 15. It offers extra practice with the logic operations, and you may find this useful.*

In this section I shall briefly introduce four logic operations. They are all very easy to perform.

Logic operations provide a useful means of accessing and manipulating an individual bit, or several bits, in a binary word. For instance, they can be used to test whether a particular bit is 1 or 0, or to ensure that a particular bit has a pre-defined value irrespective of the value of all the other bits. You will see examples of the use of logic operations later in the course; but for the present you need to concentrate on what they are and how they work.

15.1 The NOT operation

The **NOT** operation (note that, as with all logic operators, NOT is always written in capital letters) acts bit by bit on a single binary word according the following rules: **NOT**

> NOT 0 = 1
>
> NOT 1 = 0

In other words, all the 1s in the word are changed to 0s and all the 0s are changed to 1s. Hence, for example,

> NOT 1101 1011 = 0010 0100

As you saw earlier, the term *complement* or *1's complement* is sometimes used for the result of the NOT operation. In fact, you carried out the NOT operation as your first step in forming the 2's complement of a binary integer.

Another term which is used for the NOT operation, especially in electronics, is 'inversion'.

15.2 The AND operation

The **AND** operation combines two binary words bit by bit according to the rules **AND**

> 0 AND 0 = 0
>
> 0 AND 1 = 0
>
> 1 AND 0 = 0
>
> 1 AND 1 = 1

In other words, only when *both* bits are 1 is the result 1. You may find it helpful to think of it this way: when one bit is one *and* the other bit is 1 the result is 1.

Example 10

Find the result of 1101 1011 AND 1011 1010.

Answer

The bits in the two words are combined according to the above rules, working along the two words. For instance, the rightmost bit of the result is derived from 1 AND 0 = 0. Doing this for all the bits gives:

	1	1	0	1	1	0	1	1
AND	1	0	1	1	1	0	1	0
	1	0	0	1	1	0	1	0

so the result is 1001 1010.

15.3   The OR operation

The **OR** operation (occasionally called the **inclusive-OR** operation to distinguish it more clearly from the exclusive-OR operation which I shall be introducing shortly) combines binary words bit by bit according to the rules:

0 OR 0 = 0

0 OR 1 = 1

1 OR 0 = 1

1 OR 1 = 1

In other words, the result is 1 when *either* bit is 1 or when *both* bits are 1; alternatively, the result is only 0 when both bits are 0. Again, you may prefer to think of it like this: when one bit is 1 *or* the other bit is 1 the result is 1.

Example 11

Find the result of 1101 1011 OR 1011 1010.

Answer

The bits in the two words are combined according to the above rules, working along the two words. For instance, the rightmost bit of the result is derived from 1 OR 0 = 1. Doing this for all the bits gives:

	1	1	0	1	1	0	1	1
OR	1	0	1	1	1	0	1	0
	1	1	1	1	1	0	1	1

so the result is 1111 1011.

The OR operation can be used to cause a particular bit in a data word to be set to 1 when required. Think back to the way a single 8-bit word could be used to hold the seven Boolean variables that represent whether the seven segments in a 7-segment display are lit, as introduced in Section 9.5. Imagine that for some purpose the decimal point needs to be lit no matter what number is currently being displayed. The bit corresponding to the decimal point on the display is bit 0, so if an OR operation is carried out between the 8-bit word currently holding the Boolean variables for the 7-segment display and

0000 0001

then the result will be to leave the leftmost seven bits unchanged but set bit 0 to 1, which will in turn cause the decimal point to light.

15.4   The exclusive-OR operation

The **exclusive-OR** operation (usually abbreviated to **XOR**, pronounced 'ex-or') combines two binary words, bit by bit, according to the rules:

exclusive-OR
XOR

0 XOR 0 = 0

0 XOR 1 = 1

1 XOR 0 = 1

1 XOR 1 = 0

In other words, the result is 1 when either bit is 1 but not when both bits are 1 or both bits are 0, or the result is 1 when the two bits are different and 0 when they are the same.

Example 12

Find the result of 1101 1011 XOR 1011 1010.

Answer

The bits in the two words are combined according to the above rules, working along the two words. For instance, the rightmost bit of the result is derived from 1 XOR 0 = 1. Doing this for all the bits gives:

	1	1	0	1	1	0	1	1
XOR	1	0	1	1	1	0	1	0
	0	1	1	0	0	0	0	1

so the result is 0110 0001.

15.5   Summary

The logic operations introduced here are summarised in Table 1, which is an example of what is known as a 'truth table'. It shows what the result ('output') of each logic operation is for all possible combinations of 'input' values. You may find this format a useful one for remembering the various logic operations.

Table 1 Summary of the logic operations NOT, AND, OR and XOR

Operation	Inputs		Output
NOT	0	—	1
	1	—	0
AND	0	0	0
	0	1	0
	1	0	0
	1	1	1
OR	0	0	0
	0	1	1
	1	0	1
	1	1	1
XOR	0	0	0
	0	1	1
	1	0	1
	1	1	0

Activity 46 (Self assessment)

(a) If A = 0011 0111 and B = 0100 1011, find

    (i) NOT A

    (ii) A AND B

    (iii) A OR B

    (iv) A XOR B

(b) (i) Is A AND B = B AND A?

    (ii) Is A OR B = B OR A?

    (iii) Is A XOR B = B XOR A?

Comment

The answer is at the end of Block 1.

Activity 47 (Review/Exam preparation)

Now is a good point for you to turn to your *Block 1 Companion* and fill in the remaining spaces in the middle column of the tables of learning outcomes.

16 Conclusion

This block started with the idea that computers have become an important part of everyday life, especially when all the 'invisible' computers that surround us are taken into account – those embedded in objects such as kitchen scales and digital cameras. The quiz at the start of Section 3 will have brought home to you just how pervasive processors, a fundamental component of computers, now are.

Three fundamental ideas introduced in this block are:

- computers comprise both hardware (the physical objects) and software (the programs);
- computers receive data from the outside world, store it, manipulate it and present it back to the outside world;
- data in computers is represented as binary codes – that is, strings of 0s and 1s.

Figure 3 is a generic functional block diagram for a computer; it is repeated here as Figure 26. This is an important diagram in the context of the course, and you will meet it again in later blocks. Meanwhile, you have already seen it discussed in the context of the three example computers of this block: a PC, a set of digital kitchen scales and a digital camera.

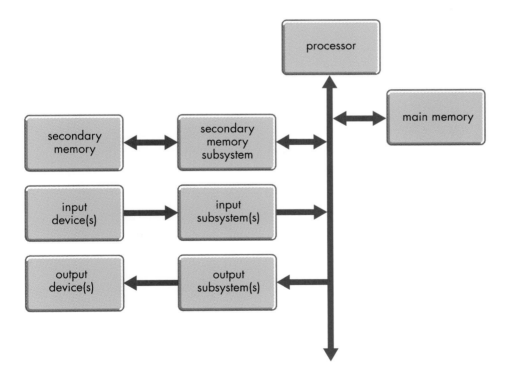

Figure 26 Repeat of Figure 3

The fundamental software components of a PC are its operating system and some application programs. Dedicated computers like those in the kitchen scales and the digital camera may well not have an operating system, but they certainly have programs to match the requirements of their applications. The tasks to be performed by these programs can be described by means of flowcharts, and you met some examples of flowcharts which describe some of the tasks performed by the three example computers of the block.

Ideas about data representation have also been applied to the three example computers, and you have seen how numbers, text, sound, pictures, analogue quantities and true/false quantities can be represented by binary codes in a computer.

You have also seen that computer instructions are represented as binary codes, and that the processor uses these binary codes to tell it what operations to perform. These operations include binary arithmetic and logic, and you have worked through some examples of both arithmetic and logic.

The rest of the course explores the ideas introduced in this block in more depth. Block 2 takes the ideas about processors and computer instructions further; Block 3 looks in some depth at embedded computers; and Block 4 focuses on PCs.

Answers to self-assessment activities

Activity 2

The keyboard and mouse relate to input devices.

The monitor and speakers relate to output devices.

To decide whether the 80 GB hard drive relates to the secondary memory, to the secondary memory subsystem or to the combination of both you need to make an intelligent guess about what those who wrote the advert meant. In this case I suspect they probably meant the combination of the two.

The 512 MB DDR RAM relates to main memory.

The DVD and the CD both relate to secondary memory.

Activity 5

The possible combinations of a 3-bit binary code are 000, 001, 010, 011, 100, 101, 110, 111. Hence the three bits can represent 8 items of data.

Activity 6

(a) Four bytes contain $4 \times 8 = 32$ bits.

(b) Since one byte contains 8 bits, the number of items that can be represented by one byte is $2^8 = 256$. (Note that if you had to work out the number of items that eight bits could represent by writing down all possible combinations of 8 bits it would be very tedious and there would be a strong possibility of making an error. Using the calculation $2^8 = 256$ is much easier way of finding the answer, as would be $2^{16} = 65\ 536$ for the number of combinations of a 16-bit binary code.)

Activity 7

The diagram is given in Figure 27.

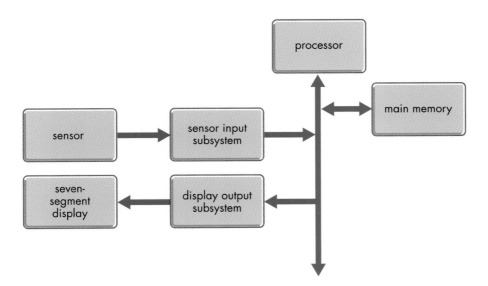

Figure 27

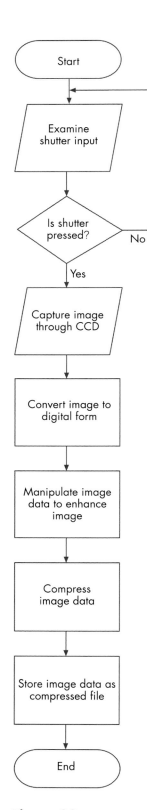

Figure 28

Activity 13

(a) The first box is the wrong shape. It refers to an input, so it should have sloping sides.

(b) The complete flowchart is shown in Figure 28. Notice that the two boxes to test whether the shutter has been pressed must come *first*, before the five boxes from Figure 11. Did you remember to write *Yes* and *No* on the appropriate branches after the decision box?

Activity 14

The flowchart is shown in Figure 29. Check that you put the boxes in the right order, that you chose the right shape for each and that you inserted *Yes* and *No* correctly after each decision box. Notice that I have started and ended this flowchart with a connector symbol. That is because it is not a self-contained program, but fits into Figure 28. Did you spot that it will fit right at the start of Figure 28, before 'Examine shutter input'? It's important to know whether flash is to be used *before* the user takes the picture!

Activity 16

The flowchart is given in Figure 30. Did you realise that the 'if' sentences need to be implemented by decision boxes? One of these starts two branches (depending on whether 'asdf' has been typed correctly) and the other a loop (to ensure that ten groups of letters are examined).

Activity 19

(a) (i)   tens (the 7 represents 70)

    (ii) thousands (there are no thousands)

    (iii) ten thousands (the 1 represents 10 000)

(b) 1

(c) $(1 \times 10^4) + (0 \times 10^3) + (2 \times 10^2) + (7 \times 10^1) + (6 \times 10^0)$

Activity 20

1010 represents

$$
\left.
\begin{array}{cccc}
2^3 & 2^2 & 2^1 & 2^0 \\
\text{eight} & \text{four} & \text{two} & \text{one} \\
1 & 0 & 1 & 0
\end{array}
\right\} \text{weightings}
$$

It is equal to $8 + 0 + 2 + 0 = 10$ in denary and its most-significant bit is 1.

Activity 21

(a) Omitting the zeros because they do not contribute to the sum, this binary number is equal to

$$(1 \times 2^7) + (1 \times 2^6) + (1 \times 2^2) + (1 \times 2^1)$$

which is $128 + 64 + 4 + 2 = 198$ in denary.

(b) In an 8-bit word the weighting of the most-significant bit is 2^7. By noting that 7 is one less than 8 you can see that the weighting of the most-significant bit in a 16-bit word will be 2^{15}. 2^{15} is equal to 32 768 and the bit number is 15 (it is the same as the exponent of 2).

(c) It is equal to

$$(1 \times 2^{15}) + (1 \times 2^0)$$

which is $32\ 768 + 1 = 32\ 769$ in denary.

Activity 22

(a) (i) 10 0000

    (ii) 1 1000

(b) 111 1111 (or 0111 1111 if an 8-bit word is to be used).

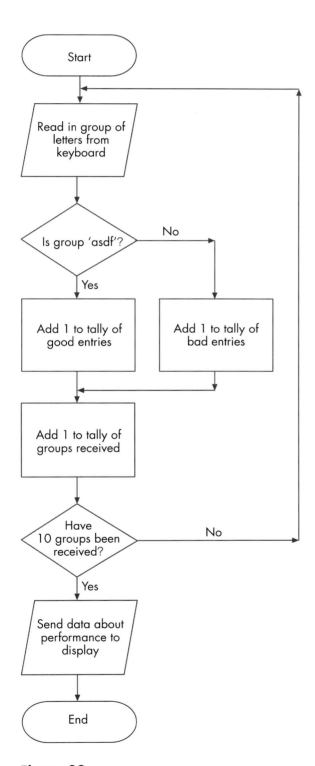

Figure 30

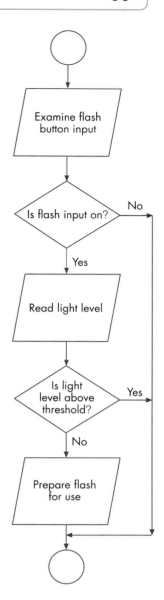

Figure 29

Activity 23

(a) Here the weightings are:

$$2^3 \quad 2^2 \quad 2^1 \quad 2^0$$
$$(8) \quad (4) \quad (2) \quad (1)$$

8, so a 0 goes into the '8' column.

Going on to the next-lower weighting, 4: 7 is larger than 4, so a 1 goes into the '4' column. The subtraction is 7 – 4, which is 3.

Continuing like this gives:

$$2^3 \quad 2^2 \quad 2^1 \quad 2^0$$
$$(8) \quad (4) \quad (2) \quad (1)$$
$$0 \quad\; 1 \quad\; 1 \quad\; 1$$

so the binary number is 0111.

(b) Here the weightings are those given in Example 1:

$$2^7 \quad\;\; 2^6 \quad\; 2^5 \quad\; 2^4 \quad\; 2^3 \quad 2^2 \quad 2^1 \quad 2^0$$
$$(128) \;\; (64) \;\; (32) \;\; (16) \;\; (8) \;\; (4) \;\; (2) \;\; (1)$$

(i) 120 is smaller than 128, so 0 goes into the '128' column. 120 is larger than 64, so a 1 goes into the '64' column. The subtraction 120 – 64 gives 56. 56 is larger than 32, so a 1 goes into the '32' column. The subtraction 56 – 32 gives 24. And so on. The result is:

$$2^7 \quad\;\; 2^6 \quad\; 2^5 \quad\; 2^4 \quad\; 2^3 \quad 2^2 \quad 2^1 \quad 2^0$$
$$(128) \;\; (64) \;\; (32) \;\; (16) \;\; (8) \;\; (4) \;\; (2) \;\; (1)$$
$$0 \quad\;\;\; 1 \quad\;\; 1 \quad\;\; 1 \quad\;\; 1 \quad\; 0 \quad 0 \quad 0$$

so the binary number is 0111 1000.

(ii) Similarly, appropriate comparisons and subtractions here give:

$$2^7 \quad\;\; 2^6 \quad\; 2^5 \quad\; 2^4 \quad\; 2^3 \quad 2^2 \quad 2^1 \quad 2^0$$
$$(128) \;\; (64) \;\; (32) \;\; (16) \;\; (8) \;\; (4) \;\; (2) \;\; (1)$$
$$0 \quad\;\;\; 0 \quad\;\; 0 \quad\;\; 0 \quad\;\; 1 \quad\; 1 \quad 0 \quad 1$$

so the binary number is 0000 1101.

Activity 25

The largest 8-bit binary number is 1111 1111. This is

$$(1 \times 128) + (1 \times 64) + (1 \times 32) + (1 \times 16) + (1 \times 8) +$$
$$(1 \times 4) + (1 \times 2) + (1 \times 1)$$

which is 255. So this is the largest positive integer than can be encoded.

Activity 28

(a) The 8-bit number is equivalent to

$$(0 \times 128) + (1 \times 64) + (0 \times 32) + (1 \times 16) + (0 \times 8) +$$
$$(1 \times 4) + (1 \times 2) + (0 \times 1)$$

which is 86 in denary.

(b) The 8-bit number is now equivalent to denary 5 then denary 6, which is denary 56.

Activity 29

(a) (i) The number is equivalent to

-2^7	2^6	2^5	2^4	2^3	2^2	2^1	2^0
(−128)	(64)	(32)	(16)	(8)	(4)	(2)	(1)
1	0	1	1	0	1	1	1

which is $-128 + 32 + 16 + 4 + 2 + 1 = -73$ in denary.

(ii) The number is equivalent to

-2^7	2^6	2^5	2^4	2^3	2^2	2^1	2^0
(−128)	(64)	(32)	(16)	(8)	(4)	(2)	(1)
0	1	0	1	1	0	1	1

which is $64 + 16 + 8 + 2 + 1 = 91$ in denary.

(b) (i) 25 is positive, so the leftmost bit is zero. The remaining 7 bits are used to represent 25, which is 001 1001 in 7-bit binary. The 8-bit 2's complement number is therefore 0001 1001.

(ii) −96 must be expressed as −128 + (a positive number); that is, as −128 + 32. The leftmost bit is 1 (representing the −128) and the remaining 7 bits are equivalent to 32, which is 010 0000. The 8-bit 2's complement number is therefore 1010 0000.

(iii) −2 is −128 + 126. The leftmost bit is 1 (representing the −128) and the remaining 7 bits are the 7-bit binary equivalent of 126, which is 111 1110. The 8-bit 2's complement number is therefore 1111 1110.

Activity 31

(a) The quantisation interval is 0.1 °C.

(b) The temperature values (in °C) could be 200.0, 200.1, 200.2, etc. up to 250.0. This is 501 possible values. Eight bits can only hold 256 different values, so 8 bits are not enough. But 9 bits can hold $2 \times 256 = 512$ bits, so 9 bits would be sufficient.

(c) The maximum possible quantisation error will occur when the actual temperature is exactly halfway between two possible values, e.g. 200.05 °C. So it is ±0.05 °C.

Activity 33

Using the same convention, the 8-bit word would be 1011 1010 because segments 7, 5, 4, 3 and 1 would be lit.

Activity 35

An image of 2272 by 1712 pixels has a total of 3 889 664 pixels. If each of these requires 30 bits, the total number of bits needed to store one picture is 116 689 920, which is 14 586 240 bytes – over 14 megabytes![9] This is why, in practice, digital cameras almost always carry out some compression before they store an image, so the image actually stored in the camera occupies less space.

---

[9] In practice, 4 bytes may be used to hold each group of 30 bits, thus increasing the amount of space needed to store one picture to an even larger value.

Activity 36

The question is: Is $2 = 3$? So the answer is: No. This is coded as follows:

　　0100 1110

　　0110 1111

　　0010 1110

You may have omitted the full stop, which is fine. If you had 'no' instead of 'No' then you will have:

　　0110 1110

　　0110 1111

Activity 37

You saw in Activity 35 that a single frame requires 14 586 240 bytes. One hundred frames therefore require 1 458 624 000 bytes if they are not compressed – over 1400 megabytes or 1.4 gigabytes!

With a JPEG compression ration of 20 this requirement would be reduced to 72 931 200 bytes; with a MPEG compression ratio of 50 this requirement would be reduced to 29 172 480 bytes.

Activity 38

(a) 5 minutes $= 300$ seconds. So there are $300 \times 40\,000$ samples. Each sample occupies 2 bytes, making a file size of $300 \times 40\,000 \times 2$ bytes, which is 24 000 000 bytes – some 24 megabytes!

(b) A sampling rate of 8000 per second will generate a fifth as many samples as a rate of 40 000 per second. So the speech file will 'only' be 4 800 000 bytes.

Activity 39

(a) In natural binary, this represents $32 + 4 = 36$.

(b) If the binary point lies between the two groups of 4 bits, then the integer part of the fraction is 0010, which is 2, and the fractional part is 0100, which is ¼. Hence the fraction is 2¼.

(c) Segments 5 and 2 are on, the others are off. Reference to Figure 21 shows that the digit 1 will be displayed.

(d) The table in the appendix of the *Reference Manual* shows that this code represents the '$' symbol.

Activity 41

(a)

```
      1   0   1   1
  +   0   0   1   1
    ─────────────────
      1   1   1   0
          1   1       (carry)
```

So the answer is 1110. Check: $1011_2 = 11_{10}$; 0011_2 is 3_{10}; 1110_2 is 14_{10}, which checks. (Note that the subscript convention is very useful here in helping to distinguish between binary and denary numbers.)

(b)

	0	1	1	0	1	1	0	0
+	0	0	0	1	0	1	1	0
	1	0	0	0	0	0	1	0
	1	1	1	1	1			(carry)

Activity 42

(a) The complement of 1010 0101 has all the 1s changed to 0s and all the 0s changed to 1s. Hence the complement is 0101 1010.

(b) The 2's complement is found by first finding the complement and then adding 1. So it is

$$0100\ 1000 + 0000\ 0001 = 0100\ 1001$$

0100 1001 is equal to 73 in denary and 1011 0111 is equal to $(-128 + 55) = -73$, which checks.

(c) Additive inverse is just another name for 2's complement, so the method is as above, giving

$$1111\ 0000 + 0000\ 0001 = 1111\ 0001$$

Activity 43

The additive inverse of the integer to be subtracted is its complement plus 1:

$$1111\ 0001 + 0000\ 0001$$

which is 1111 0010.

So the calculation is now:

	1	1	0	0	1	0	1	0
+	1	1	1	1	0	0	1	0
(1)	1	0	1	1	1	1	0	0

The ninth bit can be ignored here, as mentioned in Section 14.2. So the result is 1011 1100.

Activity 46

(a) (i) NOT A is the complement of A, which is 1100 1000.

(ii)

	0	0	1	1	0	1	1	1
AND	0	1	0	0	1	0	1	1
	0	0	0	0	0	0	1	1

So A AND B is 0000 0011.

(iii)

	0	0	1	1	0	1	1	1
OR	0	1	0	0	1	0	1	1
	0	1	1	1	1	1	1	1

So A OR B is 0111 1111.

(iv)

	0	0	1	1	0	1	1	1
XOR	0	1	0	0	1	0	1	1
	0	1	1	1	1	1	0	0

So A XOR B is 0111 1100.

(b) (i) Yes

(ii) Yes

(iii) Yes

Index of flagged terms

Acknowledgements

Grateful acknowledgement is made to the following sources for permission to reproduce material within this product.

Figures

Figure 2: From *The Guardian*, February 12th 2004; Figure 4(c): Van der Spiegel, J., 'ENIAC-on-a-chip', http://www.upenn.edu/computing/printout/archive/v12/4/chip.html. Copyright © Jan Van der Spiegel; Figure 13: Rozin, D. (2001) 'Wooden mirror', IEEE Spectrum, March 2001, p.29. Copyright © 2001 IEEE. Reprinted, with permission, from *IEEE Spectrum*, March 2001.

Every effort has been made to contact copyright holders. If any have been inadvertently overlooked the publishers will be pleased to make the necessary arrangements at the first opportunity.

Course team list

Academic staff

Bernie Clark, *Production Course Chair*

Geoff Einon

David Gorham, *Presentation Course Chair*

Reza Latif-Shabgahi

Mike Meade

Tony Nixon

Adrian Poulton

Richard Seaton

Mirabelle Walker

Production staff

Deirdre Bethune, *Course Secretary*

Colin Bluck, *Project Officer*

Annette Booz, *Compositor*

Philippa Broadbent, *Buyer, Materials Procurement*

Roger Courthold, *Graphic Artist*

Sarah Crompton, *Graphic Designer*

Daphne Cross, *Assistant Buyer, Materials Procurement*

Tony Duggan, *Learning Projects Manager*

Joanne Fellows, *QA Engineer*

Alison George, *Project Manager*

David Gosnell, *Software Designer*

Roger Harris, *Production Course Manager*

Lori Johnston, *Editor*

Karen Lemmon, *Compositor*

Deborah Mairs, *Presentation Course Manager*

Jane Moore, *Editor*

Jon Owen, *Graphic Artist*

Val Price, *Rights Executive*

Colin Thomas, *Software Designer*